Pitt Press Series

T0352030

CHAUCER

THE NONNË PRESTES TALE

CHAUCER

THE

NONNË PRESTES TALE

Edited by
LILIAN WINSTANLEY, M.A.

Cambridge:
at the University Press
1960

CAMBRIDGE UNIVERSITY PRESS
Cambridge, New York, Melbourne, Madrid, Cape Town,
Singapore, São Paulo, Delhi, Tokyo, Mexico City

Cambridge University Press
The Edinburgh Building, Cambridge CB2 8RU, UK

Published in the United States of America by
Cambridge University Press, New York

www.cambridge.org
Information on this title: www.cambridge.org/9781107648043

First published 1914
Reprinted 1923, 1926, 1940, 1948, 1950, 1960
First paperback edition 2011

A catalogue record for this publication is available from the British Library

ISBN 978-1-107-64804-3 Paperback

PREFACE

THE following text has been printed from that of the Ellesmere MS., the Chaucer Society having kindly given us permission to employ their reproduction for that purpose. I have also made certain alterations and emendations from the readings of other MSS., notably the Harleian, but they are not numerous.

I hope my study of the sources may contain a few points of general interest to Chaucerian scholars; I do not think that anyone has previously suggested the influence of "Renard le Contrefait" upon Chaucer's fable.

L. WINSTANLEY.

October 1914.

CONTENTS

INTRODUCTION

I

Chaucer and his times.

THE life of Chaucer, as generally computed, covers the years from 1300 to 1400, the latter half of the 14th century.

He is acknowledged as the father of English poetry; Spenser, himself the first of the great Elizabethans, reverenced Chaucer as his one master in the English tongue and, in attempting to complete the unfinished *Squire's Tale,* invokes him as the most 'renowned poet':

> 'Thy pardon O most sacred happie spirit
> That I thy labours lost may thus revive[1].'

As the morning star of our poetry most of Spenser's successors have hailed him. Chaucer was also the first English poet to achieve a European reputation.

Anglo-Saxon had produced a literature of its own, a literature that was really powerful and vigorous considering the period (7th to 9th centuries), but it was interrupted by the Danes who swept away Northumbrian learning and Northumbrian poetry and, as Alfred shows, almost destroyed the whole work of culture in the land ; he himself headed a prose renaissance and helped to preserve such poetry as was already in existence.

The Norman Conquest of 1066 introduced French literature as the standard and, for several centuries,

---

[1] *Faerie Queene,* IV. ii. 34.

the most fashionable writers composed in French; Anglo-French flourished greatly but it was at the cost of English literature proper which was discouraged and depressed. We possess a considerable number of English poems composed between the Conquest and the period of Chaucer but they are, for the most part, primitive in their literary method, uncertain in metre and in style. The influence of French literature becomes stronger as time proceeds; much Middle-English verse is a confusing mixture of the Anglo-Saxon alliterative and accentual type with the French type—syllabic and rhymed. The subject matter also becomes more cosmopolitan; French themes are often chosen and there is a tendency to turn to the great international cycles of Alexander, Charlemagne and Troy.

Chaucer's attitude to these different cycles varies very greatly. For the great tale of Troy he always expresses unbounded reverence (in the *Hous of Fame*, *Troilus and Criseyde*, etc.), the legends of Alexander and Charlemagne he respects but does not, except in the briefest fashion, draw upon, while for the Arthurian cycle he expresses no reverence but rather contempt.

A really great poet can hardly be produced except in a great age. However original a man's genius may be he requires a vigorous and powerful society to provide him with his material and a genuine breath of inspiration to kindle him into flame.

Chaucer, though he seems from our distance to stand so much alone, was, in reality, the product of such a distinguished age and was himself only the most eminent among numerous contemporaries.

The 14th century was a period of revival both in England and on the Continent. The first breath of the Renaissance was already kindling life in Italy and in France; the arts were reviving, great political and social changes were taking place and great religious changes were rapidly becoming inevitable. It was an age of unrest and upheaval but also of fresh, vigorous and abounding life. Even by Chaucer's time Italy had produced a number of gifted painters, sculptors and architects; among painters we may mention Cimabue and Giotto, Simone Martini, Memmi and Taddeo Gaddi; among sculptors and architects Niccolo and Giovanni Pisani, Giotto, Andrea Pisano and Andrea Orcagna.

In literature Italian achievement was even greater; in the generation before Chaucer had arisen Dante, one of the great poets of the world, the first modern to rival (as his own sure instinct made him understand) the magnificence of Virgil. Petrarch and Boccaccio were Chaucer's own contemporaries.

The study of Greek was commencing, though only just commencing, and many who would have been most zealous students were still unable to find tuition. In the person of Petrarch poetry received such honour as it had never known since the days of Augustus. And everywhere learning increased in importance: great libraries and universities were being founded, great princes became patrons of learning.

Chaucer travelled in both France and Italy; he caught their spirit, and the fresh eager delight of the early Renaissance is one of the chief fascinations of his work. In the *Clerk of Oxford* he drew the portrait of an early Renaissance scholar which may be set beside Browning's *Grammarian* as a type of the most disinterested love of learning. Oxford was, in Chaucer's time, the premier university of England; it was, intellectually and spiritually, the most keenly alive; Wyclif lived and taught there, instructing a chosen band of disciples in his religious propaganda, before addressing himself to the nation at large. Chaucer's portrait of the 'Clerk' gives us an insight into its life. The 'Clerk' lives hard and sparely, he loves the volumes of Aristotle more than rich garments or musical instruments; he lives on the gifts of patrons and gladly prays for the souls of those who give him 'wherewith to scoleye.' His figure suggests the whole democratic simplicity of the mediaeval university. So lovingly is the portrait drawn that many have seen in it an image of Chaucer in his youth. This is very possible, the more so as Chaucer makes him claim a journey to Italy and a meeting with Petrarch which was, we may be fairly sure, his own experience. There is, however, no evidence that Chaucer went to either university. What is certain is that he availed himself zealously of his resources and was, for that age, a well read and even a learned man.

He did not know Greek, but there were very few in Europe who did and he is not ashamed to confess his ignorance :

   ' But the Troyane gestes, as they felle
   In Omer, or in Dares, or in Dyte
   Who-so that can, may rede hem as they wryte[1].'

He was, however, well read in the Latin authors available in his day ; he himself names among his exemplars :

       ' Virgile, Ovyde, Lucan, and Stace,'

he translated Boethius, and to these must be added, at any rate, Cicero and Seneca. Chaucer was also well read in mediaeval Latin ; the *Wife of Bath's* Prologue and the *Nonnë Prestes Tale* in particular, mention a number of curious and out-of-the-way authors such as Nigellus Wereker, St Jerome, Dionysius Cato, Geoffrey de Vinsauf, etc., etc.

Chaucer's references to classical mythology are often quaint and peculiar, they are the references of one who relies mainly on his memory and has not a library at his back, but they serve to show what was, for the time, a great breadth of knowledge.

Chaucer was also well read in both French and Italian though here again his list is remarkable both for what it includes and for what it omits. The French poem which

[1] *Troilus and Criseyde*, I. 21.

he knew best was the great mediaeval allegory of the *Roman de la Rose* ; he translated, at any rate, a portion of this (he himself says ' all '), and he very frequently quotes from it. He was acquainted with a number of French poets forgotten to-day : such as de Deguilevile, Machault, de Gransoun and Deschamps. An eminent French critic[1] has recently pointed out that Chaucer's knowledge of mediaeval French does not include many of its best things. He did not know the finest of the old ' trouvères ' or the most primitive saint legends which are also the noblest.

' Même parmi les romans en vers, les plus beaux lui échappèrent ; rien ne permet de supposer qu'il ait connu Chrestien de Troyes[2].'

No doubt the secret of Chaucer's contempt for the romances is to be found in the fact that he only knew the later and more degenerate forms.

The great Italians he loved well. He refers to Dante with humility and reverence and there are many quotations from him in the *Hous of Fame*. His *Clerk of Oxford* claims to have learnt the tale of Griselda at Padua directly from the lips of Petrarch :

> ' Fraunceys Petrark, the laureate poete,
> Hightè this clerk, whos rethoryke sweete
> Enlumined al Itaille of poetrye.'

Boccaccio was, however, the Italian writer to whom Chaucer owed most ; curiously enough Chaucer never refers to him by name nor is there any proof that he was acquainted with Boccaccio's chief work—the *Decameron* ; the latter did not, however, stand out as prominently for the men of the 14th century as it does for us. Boccaccio's own age seems to have admired him as a poet rather than as a prose-writer and Chaucer appears to have followed the ordinary bent of his time ; two of his most important works—*Troilus and Criseyde*

---

[1] Legouis' *Chaucer.*　　　　　[2] *Ibid.*

and the *Knight's Tale*—are adaptations of Boccaccio, taken respectively from the *Filostrato* and the *Teseide*.

The writer whom Chaucer reverenced most was Virgil, but those who had the most powerful influence over his maturer work were Boccaccio and Ovid, probably because their talents were more essentially akin to his own; they are both great ' raconteurs,' among the greatest in the world, and that was also Chaucer's gift. Dante and Petrarch he could love and reverence, but the intense spirituality of the one, the subjectivity of the other, were alike foreign to his genius.

Chaucer, it should be observed, had in him the making of a man of science. He was well acquainted with the one real science of his time—that of astronomy. He translated a treatise on the Astrolabe—an astronomical instrument; he uses astronomical references to give notes of time and they are generally exact and careful.

On the negative side Chaucer also shows a scientific frame of mind by the vast number of things, usually credited in his day, in which he does *not* believe. The scientific mind begins, as a rule, with scepticism, in a clearing of the ground from errors. In Chaucer's day the majority were quite extraordinarily credulous; they believed in the most fantastic saint legends, in alchemy, the transmutation of metals into gold; they believed in the power of divining by dreams, and their so-called ' medicine' was, for the most part, a mixture of false physiology, astrology and herbalism. At all these things Chaucer laughed with thorough-going scepticism, too amiable to be bitter, but caustic, clear-sighted and cold. In the prologue to the *Pardoner's Tale* he gives a drastic exposure of the superstitions associated with relics :

> ' Than shewe I forth my longe cristal stones,
> Y-crammed ful of cloutes and of bones ;
> Reliks been they, as wenen they echoon.'

In the *Chanoun's Yeoman's Tale* he presents a most

convincing and detailed satire upon the pretences of alchemy and, as we shall see, in the *Nonnë Prestes Tale* and elsewhere, he mocks at mediaeval medicine and the art of divining by dreams.

Occasionally his scepticism goes so far as to encroach upon his art. Thus, in the *Franklin's Tale* he has to describe how a certain ' tregetour ' or juggler makes it appear as if all the rocks on the coast of Brittany were ' away.' This is absolutely necessary to the plot, but Chaucer cannot forbear from expressing his contempt for the whole business and especially for the magic book :

> ' Whiche book spak muchel of the operaciouns,
> Touchinge the eighte and twenty mansiouns
> That longen to the mone, and swich folye,
> As in our dayes is nat worth a flye.'

Even if we did not know it from any other source we should gather from Chaucer's pages that the 14th century was an age of reviving art ; he speaks of paintings and sculptures with such passionate love and always, it is to be noted, as if they were rare and wonderful things, almost miraculous. He has much of that spirit which, as we hear from Vasari, would make a whole Italian town turn out in procession and festival to receive some painting by Cimabue or Giotto. We may instance the paintings on the wall which Chaucer describes in the *Hous of Fame* and the gorgeous account of the three temples in the *Knight's Tale*. These are the representations of Venus :

> ' The statue of Venus, glorious for to see,
> Was naked fleting in the large see,
> And fro the navele down all covered was
> With waves grene, and brighte as any glas.
> A citole in hir right hand hadde she,
> And on hir heed, ful semely for to see,
> A rose gerland, fresh and wel smellinge,
> Above hir heed hir dowves flikeringe ;
> Biforn hir stood hir sone Cupido
> Up-on his shuldres winges hadde he two ;
> And blind he was, as it is often sene ;
> A bowe he bar and arwes brighte and kene ! '

and of Diana :

> ' This goddesse on an hert ful hye sect,
> With smale houndes al aboute hir fect,
> And undernethe hir feet she hadde a mone,
> Wexing it was, and sholde wanie sone.
> In gaude grene hir statue clothed was
> With bowe in hand and arwes in a cas.'

It is impossible to come across such descriptions without perceiving the resemblance between them and the early mythological paintings of Italy, such, for instance, as those in the palaces of Ferrara.

Chaucer's Theseus has the same zest and eagerness in patronising art as that shown by Italian nobles :

> ' For in the lond ther nas no crafty man,
> That geometrie or ars-metrik can,
> Ne purtreyour, ne kerver of images,
> That Theseus ne yaf him mete and wages
> The theatre for to maken and devyse.'

Chaucer's age showed the first breath of the Renaissance in its love of learning and love of art ; he himself, as we have seen, is deeply impressed by both ; he shows the Renaissance love of learning, its passion for books and knowledge, its enquiring, sceptical, scientific temper, its intense love of art and beauty.

Let us ask next how Chaucer is related to the great national and social movements of his day.

The latter half of the 14th century was a most interesting and significant period in English history. The reign of Edward III was a really great reign, marked by the brilliant victories gained against Scotland and France, by Crecy and Poictiers, by the captivities of King John of France and Robert Bruce.

Chaucer grew to manhood in a period of national triumph and there can be little doubt that the literary activity of the 14th century can be traced very largely to the national success in war. The triumph over France inspired the poetry of that age precisely as the heroic and triumphant struggle against Spain inspired

the poetry of the Elizabethan period. The joy and
gladness that is so manifest a characteristic of Chaucer,
his satisfaction with the world, his confidence that life,
in spite of all its disillusions and drawbacks, is still
an excellent thing—are the spirit of a thriving and
triumphing nation as England certainly was in his youth.
Chaucer must, however, have been of an optimistic
temper, for we cannot trace any change of tone in his
work ; before the end of his life he saw plenty of gloom,
the sordid close of a mighty reign, the vast and tragic
disasters which gathered around the course of Richard II.
This period is not reflected at all in Chaucer's work, he
ignores its stress and gloom; in the pages of his great
contemporary Langland we can see, as is so often the
case, exactly the side that Chaucer omitted ; Langland
mirrors for us the harpy-like greed of Alice Perrers,
Edward III's mistress, the doubts and terrors that
surrounded the opening reign of a child, the depression
that followed the war.

Another fact, equally remarkable, is that Chaucer
says not a word against France. He himself served in
the ill-fated expedition of 1359, he was taken prisoner
and remained in captivity for nearly a year. It was
an age of fierce and bitter partisanship and both French
and English were accustomed to inveigh against each
other in violent terms. Froissart is wrathful and furious
against the English ; Chaucer's fellow-countryman—
Lawrence Minot—is foul-mouthed and savage in his
abuse of the French. But Chaucer has no sign of
animosity ; indeed he hardly refers to the conflict ; he
mentions the fact that his squire had served in ' Artoys
and Picardye ' but he says no more.

He often refers to French literature and French poets
with the sweetest courtesy, as when he speaks of Graun-
soun, ' flour of hem that make in France,' but there is
not a word against their country.   Are we to set it down
to his love of French literature, to his recognition of the

debt he owed their poets, or simply to his natural sweet-ness of disposition? Whatever the explanation, the fact remains. He is of the mood of Sir Philip Sidney when the latter praised 'that sweet enemy, France.' The earliest of our great poets, Chaucer is one of the least insular.

In home affairs again the age was one of varied activity and rapid change. The preaching of Wyclif stirred the whole nation and heralded the Reformation.

In religious matters Chaucer is truly a mirror of his time. His great patron, John of Gaunt, was also a patron of Wyclif, defended and maintained him against his enemies; Chaucer evidently followed the whole con-troversy with the keenest interest.

It is surprising how many of the Wyclifite 'points' are illustrated by Chaucer. Wyclif began his career as a theologian by following up the great Augustinian con-troversy started by Thomas afterwards Bishop Brad-wardine, on the subject of predestination versus free-will.

Wyclif worked his way round to a belief in predesti-nation, in this as in so many other things anticipating Puritanism. This question was Chaucer's favourite philo-sophical problem, and, as we shall see, in the *Nonnĕ Prestes Tale* he makes a very plain reference to Wyclif's charac-teristic doctrine of the 'foresciti' or 'foreknown.'

Wyclif was a life-long opponent of Rome and its malign and evil influence; he objected to the jurisdiction of the ecclesiastical courts. Chaucer represents, among the very worst of his rogues, the Pardoner and Sum-moner; the Pardoner, the most dangerous of all his scoundrels, has his wallet

'Bret-ful of pardons, come from Rome al hoot.'

Wyclif especially hated 'indulgences,' and in the *Pardoner's* prologue Chaucer explains, or rather makes his rogue explain, with what unbridled effrontery the sale of such indulgences was carried on. Wyclif preached against the worship of relics and Chaucer tells us of the glass crammed full of ' pigges bones.'

Wyclif complained that the monks, notwithstanding all their enormous landed wealth, had become practically useless members of society, who did nothing for the nation in return for the immense revenues they enjoyed, and Chaucer gives us his ironical picture of the hunting monk whose whole life is in the chase, who spends all his time ' pricking and hunting for the hare.'

Wyclif preached against the mendicant friars, saying they had become idle, corrupt and mischievous, careless in their methods of dealing with the sins of the laity, giving short shrift and swift absolution ; Chaucer presents us with the portrait of the ' limitour ' in which all these traits are depicted with matchless skill :

> ' Ful swetely herde he confessioun
> And plesaunt was his absolucioun.'

Wyclif disliked excommunication, he defied its power when it was uttered upon himself, and he doubted Rome's power of absolution ; Chaucer jeers at both :

> ' For curs will slee right as assoiling saveth[1].'

Wyclif pointed out the many short-comings and fail-ings of the parish priest and founded his own order of ' poor priests ' to show what such men should be like. Chaucer's ' Poor Persoun of a Toun ' is plainly meant as a picture of one of these ; everywhere in his portrait we see the poet contrasting him with the careless type which was common ; he does *not* ' cursen for his tithes,' he does *not* leave his flock ' encombred in the myre ' and go to London to seek a chantry, etc., etc. If we had any doubt about the identification it would be removed by the host—Hary Bailly—who accuses the ' Persoun ' of being a Lollard which the latter does not attempt to deny[2].

[1] Prologue.
[2] *Shipman's* Prologue.

As the schism widened between Wyclif and the University of Oxford the great reformer turned more and more to the ignorant and unlearned, he preached mainly to them and relied mainly on them. Chaucer, in the whole of his motley crowd, represents the ' Persoun ' and his brother the ' Plowman ' as being by far the truest and most zealous Christians. The whole Wyclifite controversy is very thoroughly mirrored in Chaucer's pages, and this is the more remarkable as it seems to be the only great contemporary quarrel of which he took much note.

The reigns of Edward III and Richard II were periods of great constitutional change. The outstanding features of the time were the continual growth in power of the Commons and the bitter revolts of the peasant labourers. To these affairs Chaucer pays no heed. He was himself, about the time when he commenced the *Canterbury Tales*, knight of the shire for Kent, but we could never discover, we could not even guess from his pages, that the latter half of the 14th century was one of the great parliamentary periods of English history. It is true that there are ' parlements ' in Chaucer ; by a most curious anachronism he introduces one into the *Knight's Tale*, where Theseus summons his ' counseil and his baronage ' to advise him in arranging a royal marriage. A parliamentary debate is also mocked at, very skilfully and ingeniously, in the *Parlement of Foules*, but there is no serious treatment of the subject. Chaucer's omission is the more striking because Langland speaks continually of the Commons, in *Piers Plowman* he is always discussing the growing power of the Commons, whether it is for good or ill, how far it ought to entrench upon the royal prerogative, where its limits should be ; Langland's very description of a king is ' might of the communes made him to reigne.'

There are, however, several reasons which may help to explain why Chaucer did not show himself sympa-

thetic to Parliaments. That very Parliament of 1386
in which he took his seat attacked fiercely and obsti-
nately the powers of his patron John of Gaunt; the
friends of Lancaster, Chaucer among them, must have
had an unpleasant experience. Again the Parliaments
of Edward III represented mainly the growing power
of the middle class, the bourgeoisie, and it was precisely the section of the nation which Chaucer liked
least. Chaucer had strong aristocratic sympathies and
strong democratic sympathies but the middle class he
regarded, judging from the types he has given, as being
self-seeking and self-centred, devoid alike of principle
and of honour. It is noticeable that nearly all his best
characters are either aristocrats like the Knight and the
Squire or quite poor people like the Clerk, the Persoun
and the Plowman. Chaucer admires the chivalrous
ideal, the scholarly ideal, the religious ideal (when
genuine), but for the money-making, commercial ideal
he has nothing but ironic contempt; he was well aware
of the growing power of the middle class—there are many
proofs of that in his pages—but he scorns their standards
and is amused by their pretensions.

The Merchant is continually talking of gain; he is
really in debt though he conducts himself so cleverly
that no one guesses it, and Chaucer finishes up by a
significant and contemptuous touch in forgetting his
name:

'But sooth to seyn, I noot how men him calle.'

Concerning his group of mechanics he tells us care-
fully how prosperous they are, but he finds something
irresistibly comic in their idea of civic dignities, their
chief ambition being to sit 'in a yeldhalle on a deys'
and their wives also dream of having 'a mantel regal-
liche y-bore.' He does not refer to them again nor does
he make any of them tell tales.

As for the professions, Chaucer, like a distinguished
modern author, seems to regard them as being essentially

'conspiracies against the public.' The Man of Lawe, Chaucer tells us, is of ' greet reverence ' and then adds immediately ' He seemed such, his wordes weren so wyse,' while the Doctour is plainly a charlatan and a solemn fraud with more than a touch of avarice :

> ' For gold in phisik is a cordial
> Therefore he lovede gold in special.'

It is the lower middle class, however, upon whom Chaucer, like Langland, is the most severe ; he shows us many examples but he regards them all as being essentially dishonest ; they rob their employers whenever they get the chance, feathering their nest at the cost of those who are foolish enough to trust them ; they betray confidence with cynical impudence ; they all (and here Chaucer is at one with the sad bitterness of Langland) brutally ill-treat the poor who fall into their power : the Miller steals flour and takes thrice his dues and yet is honest as millers go, the farm-bailiffs and labourers were afraid of the Reve :

> ' They were adrad of him, as of the deeth,'

and the Shipman, the master-mariner, is the worst of all, for he plays pirate whenever he gets the chance and drowns the crews of any ships he takes :

> ' By water he sent hem hoom to every lond.'

Concerning the ' people ' as such, the labourers, the class who were hardly better than serfs, Chaucer seems to have known but little. They are the only class unrepresented in his gallery of pilgrims. We learn much of them from Langland who knew them well and who often speaks of their unremunerative toil, their poverty and their sufferings, but Chaucer scarcely refers to them. Towards the ' Peasants' Revolt ' he was not, apparently, sympathetic. He alludes to it contemptuously in the *Nonnĕ Prestes Tale* where the pursuers of the fox shout as loudly as Jack Straw and his ' meynee,' ' when they would a Fleming kill.'

It was only natural that Chaucer should dislike the narrow-mindedness and cruelty by which the revolt was accompanied. The rebels in 1381 showed a fierce hatred of foreigners, and murderous assaults on Flemings and Lombards were a marked feature of the insurrection. There were a number of Flemings who had established themselves under the government to pursue the woollen industry and, oblivious of their great value to the country as a whole, the poor persisted in regarding them mainly as rivals to native weavers; 34 Flemish weavers were murdered in a batch at the church of St Martin's Vintry.

Chaucer may have heard the very cries that he himself describes.

We may remember, in this connection also, that the animosity of the rebels was directed very largely against John of Gaunt and that they burnt and sacked his palace of the Savoy, the finest private residence in England.

We have already remarked the fact that Chaucer belonged to an age of literary revival. He was the chief poet of his time, but he had a number of contemporaries by no means negligible. Fourteenth century literature is, in fact, very rich and varied; its most distinctive features are its division into a number of different ' schools ' based on differences of dialect and its tentative and experimental character. There was, as yet, no standard English.

The part played by Northumbrian in the 7th and 8th centuries, by West Saxon in the 9th and 10th, was not, in Chaucer's time, filled by any one dialect.

French had for several centuries been the standard literary language, and it was only in the reign of Edward III that English became the accepted tongue of the whole nation and was substituted for French in the law-courts and schools; moreover the French war, by bringing the two countries into sharp antagonism, had caused French to become, in a manner, unpatriotic; for the first time it was possible for a court poet to write in English. Chaucer, with instinctive tact, and probably also with love for his native language, availed himself of the opportunity, though it was not until his success was indisputable that his companion poet—Gower—did the same.

The Middle English of Chaucer's time falls into four main dialects : (1) the Northern, (2) the West Midland, (3) the East Midland, (4) the Southern or Kentish. These dialects were lineally descended from Anglo-Saxon dialects and they had, all of them, altered considerably in the lapse of centuries.

Anglo-Saxon was a highly-inflected language, resembling modern German. Owing to the influence of the Danes the shedding of inflections began and proceeded very rapidly in the north where the niceties of Anglo-Saxon grammar were soon lost; the same process continued all over the country after the Conquest. The northern dialect adopted very freely Scandinavian loanwords and all of the dialects borrowed much from French.

The northern dialect had a wide range, stretching from the Humber to Aberdeen. In the 14th century it possessed two important writers—the Scottish Barbour and the English Lawrence Minot. The fierce struggles of the Scotch and English occupy both of these though, naturally, from opposite points of view. Barbour's *Bruce* (dated about 1375) is a fine patriotic poem ; it is not of much value historically since it admits legend as freely as fact, but it gives a romantic and impassioned view of the great struggle of Scotland against Edward I. The poem is inspired by a really noble spirit of liberty and its motto might be stated in its own words :

> ' A ! fredome is a noble thing !
> Fredome all solace to man giffis.
> He levys at ease that frely levys.'

Servitude is more horrible than death for it mars the whole man ' body and bones,' while death ' annoys ' him but once.

Lawrence Minot composed a number of war-songs and war-poems ; he celebrates the victories of Edward III against the French and Scotch ; his songs were probably written between 1333 and 1352 about the same time as the different events they celebrate : Halidon Hill, Crecy, Sluys, etc. Minot's poems are somewhat rough ; they are written in end-rhyme with a considerable amount of alliteration, but they are very vigorous, possessing the inevitable force of a writer dealing with great contemporary events in the white-hot spirit of the moment.

The West Midland dialect stretched west of the Pennines ; like the Northern it possessed several distinct schools of writers.

In the counties of Lancashire and Cheshire the population had, probably, a large admixture of Celtic blood and close connections with the Welsh across the Border ; the subject matter of their poets is, not infrequently, taken from Arthurian legend. The most remarkable is the beautiful anonymous poem, written in alliterative measure, which is known as *Sir Gawayne and the Grene Knight*. The ' Gawayne ' poet stands nearer to Chaucer in genius than any other writer of the day. The excellences of the work are many : it is a genuine Celtic romance, revealing the Celtic spirit of adventure, full of Celtic purity, delicacy and chivalry. The poem may be compared, as a romance, with Chaucer's *Troilus and Criseyde* or his *Knight's Tale* or his *Squire's Tale*.

There is the same subtle and delicate psychology as in *Troilus* ; the description of Sir Gawayne in his armour may be set, in its splendour and beauty, beside the pictures of Emetreus and Lycurgus in the *Knight's Tale* : the opening scene is as marvellous and as well thought out as the opening of the *Squire's Tale* : it tells how Arthur is holding his great yearly festival when an enchanter, clad all in green and riding upon a green horse, rides up to his board and challenges any of the knights present to exchange blows with him ; all are silent, fearing the manifest strangeness of the adventure, and Arthur is about to accept the challenge himself when Gawayne steps forth, accepts the conditions and strikes off at one blow the head of the stranger knight who proceeds to pick up his head, makes an appointment for a year and a day from that date, and rides out with his head in his hand. Nothing could be better told, and not Chaucer himself could carry us more wonderfully to the heart of fairyland. Like Chaucer again the Gawayne poet excels in describing nature and with an even wider variety; he has a keen eye for colour, a delicate and masterly touch; he depicts, which is very rare in mediaeval poets, both mountain scenery and winter storm.

The southern variety of the West Midland dialect had its centre in Shropshire; its chief poet was William Langland, who is known by his one extensive poem of *Piers Plowman*. This work exists in three forms, usually known as the A, B, and C texts; recent criticism inclines to the view that the three texts may be by different authors[1]. The B text is considerably the best.

From the strictly literary point of view *Piers Plowman* is inferior to *Sir Gawayne*, for its writer has nothing like the same narrative talent or sense of beauty, but he was a man of deep moral fervour and he wrote with burning intensity of feeling upon most of the disputed questions of the day. His poem was certainly one of the most popular in the 14th century for we possess an extraordinary number of MSS.

Piers Plowman is a long religious allegory divided into many separate visions: the hero—Piers Plowman—is the ideal labourer, simple, hard-working and unassuming, the man who is the foundation of society, the true Christian who ultimately becomes, by a stroke of supreme daring, the revelation of the divine in man—Christ him-

---

[1] Professor Manly, *Camb. Hist. of Eng. Lit.* vol. II.

self.   Langland expresses most powerfully the spirit of
social unrest as it existed in the 14th century ; he is
the voice of all that seething revolt which surged in
the Peasants' Rebellion, in John Ball, in Wat Tyler and
the rest of the rebel leaders.

Little is known of his life and that little is gathered
doubtfully from the pages of his book ; he was certainly
poor, and the stratum of society which he knew best
was the one which, as we have seen, Chaucer knew least
—the poorest labouring class.   Langland is by no means
blind to their faults : their recklessness when they do
obtain money, their extravagance and drunkenness, but
he also passionately sympathises with them because they
pay the penalty for all ; the labourer is the base of the
social pyramid and he pays not only for his own faults
and shortcomings (which might be just), but for the
faults and shortcomings of all the others.

It is impossible to read Langland without being
startled by the many affinities between him and modern
Socialism.   William Morris was well justified when, in
his *Dream of John Ball*, he stated his own ideals as the
vision of a 14th century reformer.

It is in his attitude to religion and the religious orders
that Langland has most in common with Chaucer ; the
picture he gives of their corruption is essentially the
same, though he differs, of course, in details.   He is
somewhat less severe upon the monks than Chaucer but
much harder on the nuns ; he makes a similarly drastic
attack upon summoners, friars and pardoners and adds
a bitter anger against hermits and pilgrims.

Indeed, as a commentary upon Chaucer, Langland
is throughout invaluable ; he shows us so often the
obverse of Chaucer's medal.

Chaucer represents his Knight and Squire pursuing
their high ideals abroad, in Lithuania and Prussia,
Picardye and elsewhere, and Langland shows what it
all came to for the poor tenants left without defence

at home, victimised by the rapacity of robbers and a prey to the extortions of unscrupulous agents.

Chaucer describes for us the Man of Law—powerful, important and excellently thriving, and Langland shows us what his prosperity meant for the poor man who invariably found the lawyer against him, ready to juggle away his rights, and who could not himself get 'a mum of his mouth' were he never so oppressed.

Chaucer gives us a drastic picture of the extortion and meanness, the general dishonesty of the bourgeoise class, and Langland calls on the king and commons to make laws to punish severely the

'Brewsteres and bakesteres[1] . bocheres and cokes;
For thise aren men on this molde[2]. þat most harme worcheth
To the pore peple . that parcel-mele buggen[3].'[4]

He tells us indignantly that they buy 'rentes,' they 'build high' by poisoning the food and pinching the bellies of the poorest of the poor.

Elsewhere[5] he shows us how the cheating is carried on, how ten or twelve yards of cloth are stretched out to thirteen, how false scales are employed and how the labourer is cheated even in his ale:

'Peny-ale and podyng-ale[6] . she poured togidres[7].'

A typical example of Langland's middle-class is the innkeeper who, on being told that 'restitution' would be proper for him, at once understands it to be the French word for robbery[8].

Langland's poem is written in the Anglo-Saxon alliterative measure which was, with him, a deliberate literary revival.

The East Midland dialect was the tongue of the Universities and of London ; it would probably, in any case, have become the literary language, but Chaucer's own writings helped to give it predominance. Its leading

[1] Bakers.   [2] Earth.   [3] Who buy in small quantities.
[4] *Piers Plowman*, Passus III.   [5] Passus V.
[6] Of poor quality.   [7] Passus V.   [8] Passus V.

writers were Chaucer and Gower. Gower was also a court poet and his literary history shows the unsettled fashions of the time, for he wrote a long poem in Latin and one in French before turning to English. His English poem, the *Confessio Amantis*, was probably suggested by the success of the *Canterbury Tales*. It consists of a series of stories in a common framework, but Gower, though he has his graces, is no rival to Chaucer and is, in pure literary talent, far inferior to Langland and the Gawayne poet.

Interesting as are the other 14th century writers Chaucer is, beyond comparison, the greatest English poet of his day. He owes his achievement mainly to the fact that he perceived what his fellow-poets did not—the necessity for real literary canons, for true artistic form and greatness of conception. He realised that his own country and contemporaries had comparatively little to offer and he turned to the literatures which were then the best in Europe—the French and the Italian. He learnt from the Italians especially the secret of noble construction and of imperishable style. It is by his style mainly that he stands pre-eminent among the men of his time. His English contemporaries have many virtues but they never catch the accent of the world's great poetry which, when he has once learnt his art, comes so naturally and so inevitably to Chaucer.

No other English poet before him can show such lines as :

> ' Singest with vois memorial in the shade
> Under the laurer which that may not fade[1],'

or,

> ' The smyler with the knyf under the cloke[2],'

or,

> ' What is this world ? what asketh men to have,
> Now with his love, now in his colde grave,
> Alone withouten any compagnye[3],'

[1] *Anelida and Arcite.*   [2] *Knight's Tale.*   [3] *Ibid.*

or,

> ' O gode god ! how gentle and how kind
> You semed by your speche and your visage
> The day that maked was our mariage[1].'

There is no mistaking the accent of such—their high dignity, their easy mastery, their lingering haunting beauty.

And Chaucer is no less a master of irony and humour than of dignity and pathos; even the brilliant 18th century writers seem hard and epigrammatic, a trifle mechanical when compared with the finished urbane perfection of Chaucer's wit.

What could be more perfect than the whole description of the ' Frere ' :

> ' He was an esy man to yeve penaunce
> Ther as he wiste to han a good pitaunce,'

or than the bitter lament of the Merchant when he has just heard of the woes of Griselda ?

> ' Ther is a long and large difference
> Bitwix Grisildis grete pacience
> And of my wyf the passing crueltee[2].'

And Chaucer's humour is everywhere ; it is the magic atmosphere which seems to bathe all his poetry as with sharp, clear light. It is the main secret of his incomparable vividness.

The circumstances of Chaucer's life were such as to bring him into contact with men and affairs and to take him frequently abroad. We know more of his life than of most mediaeval poets because he was engaged most of his time in the public service and thus we are able to find information in public records.

The date of his birth is doubtful but is usually fixed about 1340. Chaucer gave evidence in the Scrope and Grosvenor trial of 1386 ; he is there described as being ' forty years of age and upwards ' (XL ans et plus) and it is further stated that he had borne arms for 27 years.

---

[1] *Clerk's Tale.*   [2] *Merchant's* Prologue.

The ages given in the Scrope and Grosvenor trial are (as can be proved from other sources) very often inaccurate; most of them, moreover, are in round numbers which suggests that they were not taken from the statements of the witnesses themselves but were rather the guesses of an official who estimated the age of witnesses from their appearance. However, if Chaucer were born in 1340, he would have entered military service at the age of 19 which was about the usual time. Other evidence points in the same direction and we may assume that Chaucer was born between 1340 and 1344, the earlier date being probably more nearly correct.

The poet was the son of John Chaucer a vintner of Thames Street, London, and his father appears to have had some link with the royal household.

Our first authentic notice of Chaucer is to be found in the year 1357; in the household accounts of Elizabeth, wife of Lionel, Duke of Clarence, mention is made of clothes provided for a certain Geoffrey Chaucer, who was a page in her service and who accompanied her during her residences at Hatfield and elsewhere. The identification is, of course, not absolutely certain, but there is every probability that this Geoffrey Chaucer was the poet. It is worthy of note that John of Gaunt was a frequent visitor at Hatfield and may when there have made the poet's acquaintance.

Two years later, in 1359, came the ill-fated expedition to France in which Chaucer served; we know from his own evidence, in the Scrope and Grosvenor trial, that he was taken prisoner. He was ransomed in March, 1360, shortly before the treaty of Bretigny, the king himself subscribing £16 (about £200 in our money) which may have been the whole sum.

We have no means of knowing how Chaucer fared during his imprisonment but, as we have seen, he has not a word to utter against the French and this in itself implies that he was not harshly treated.

Indeed it is possible that his imprisonment may have actually helped him in his literary work by increasing his knowledge of French poetry.

He probably entered the king's service as a valet shortly afterwards, though we have no record of him for the next seven years ; in 1367 Edward III awarded him an annuity of 20 marks for life, terming him ' dilectus valettus noster.'

In 1366 we find Chaucer already married. On Sep. 12th in that year a certain Philippa Chaucer, described as ' una domicellarum camerae Philippae Reginae Angliae,' received a pension from the queen, and in the year 1381 this pension was confirmed by Richard II and paid through her husband Geoffrey Chaucer.

It has been conjectured that the poet's wife was Philippa Roet, daughter of Sir Payne Roet, Guienne King of Arms ; in that case she would be the sister of Katharine Swynford, who became the third wife of John of Gaunt, and the fact would help to explain the undoubtedly close connection between Chaucer and the house of Lancaster, for the poet's fortunes invariably rose and fell with those of John of Gaunt.

In 1369 Chaucer again joined the army in France.

In the same year a great pestilence ravaged England ; among those who perished, probably of the plague, was Blanche of Lancaster, the first wife of John of Gaunt, a lady whose memory the poet honoured in the *Book of the Duchesse*.

From 1370 to 1386 Chaucer was attached to the court and employed on various diplomatic services ; he must have been an excellent man of affairs or he would not have been trusted with so many important and confidential missions.

Incidentally his missions gave him the opportunity of travel and of familiarising himself with the world. In 1372 he was sent with two other commissioners (one a Genoese subject) to treat with the republic of Genoa concerning the establishment of a trading centre in England. He was probably selected because of his knowledge of Italian. He remained in Italy for nearly a year and his great interest in Italian literature is usually dated from this period.

In 1374 Chaucer received the important office of Comptroller of the Wool Customs for the Port of London. It was his duty to write the rolls of the office with his own hand, to be continually present and to perform his work personally. In 1375 he received from the crown the custody of the lands and person of Edward, a minor, son and heir of Edward Staplegate of Kent. Such wardships were offices of profit.

In 1376 Sir John Burley and Geoffrey Chaucer were employed on some secret service, the nature of which is unknown.

In 1377 Chaucer was sent on a secret mission to Flanders.

Edward III died in 1377 but the poet still remained in favour and his employments did not lessen ; in the next year he was despatched on two important missions ; the first, in company with three knights, was to negotiate for the marriage of Richard II to a French princess, but the project came to nothing ; he was also despatched on a second visit to Italy, accompanying Sir Edward Berkeley on a mission to Bernabo Visconti of Milan, to treat of certain matters touching the king's expedition of war (pro certis negociis expeditionem guerre regis tangentibus)—a phrase of uncertain meaning.

In 1382 Richard II was married to Anne of Bohemia ; she proved one of the noblest of English queens, was greatly beloved and a patroness of poetry and learning. She seems to have shown much kindness to the poet who addresses her with genuine gratitude.

In 1382 Chaucer received a second office—Comptroller of the Petty Customs—for the Port of London, which office he was permitted to exercise by deputy. It is remarkable that none of Chaucer's predecessors had been so favoured and it is also remarkable that he was the only man who held the two Comptrollerships simultaneously ; his tenure of office was also unusually long[1]. All these facts go to confirm us in the belief that Chaucer must have been an unusually good man of business.

In 1385 he experienced a further stroke of good fortune in being allowed to perform the duties of his first office also by deputy ; this was a very rare and remarkable favour and it has been conjectured that he owed it to the good offices of the queen who desired to give him more leisure for poetic composition ; what is certain is that he wrote the *Legend of Good Women* in her honour, apparently to thank her for some signal favour.

In the year 1386 Chaucer was elected knight of the shire for Kent and sat, as we know from the record of his travelling expenses thither, in that very Parliament which attacked the powers of his patron—John of Gaunt. The Duke of Gloucester received the supreme control and Chaucer soon felt the effect of this ascendency, for in Dec. 1386 he was deprived of both his Comptrollerships though he retained his own and his wife's pensions. In 1387 his wife's pension was paid for the last time ; in all probability she died in that year.

The period during which John of Gaunt was absent in Spain (1386–89) seems to have been a time of distress and even penury for Chaucer, for we find him commuting his pensions for ready money, thus capitalising his income ; they were assigned to a certain John Scalby. These years must, however, have been a time of leisure and probably included a good deal of his work upon the *Canterbury Tales*.

In 1389 the king (Richard II) by a *coup d'état* took the government into his own hands ; John of Gaunt returned soon afterwards, was once more received into

[1] See ' Studies in the Life Records of Chaucer,' S. Moore, *Anglia*, vol. xxv.

favour, and Chaucer also experienced an accession of good fortune. He was appointed Clerk of the King's Works at Westminster and elsewhere. This again was a rare privilege, for most of the persons so appointed were 'king's clerks' and Chaucer appears to have been the only layman who held the office[1].

In 1390 he was appointed, with five others, on a commission to repair the banks of the Thames between Woolwich and Greenwich, but in 1391 he once more fell into misfortune and lost his public offices.

During the later years of Chaucer's life he seems to have been in frequent straits for money, for we find him several times making applications for his pensions to be paid in advance and the sums he asks for are at times most pitifully small; we find also that the king grants him letters of protection against creditors.

In 1399 Richard II was deposed and Henry IV succeeded. The accession of a Lancastrian king, the son of his old patron, was a stroke of great good luck for Chaucer who addressed a poetic appeal at once to Henry, the verses entitled *Compleynt to his Empty Purs*. He received an immediate response for, only four days after his accession, Henry, who probably knew him personally, doubled the poet's pension.

Chaucer did not long enjoy this revival of good fortune; he died in the next year, the second of Henry's reign; his tombstone in Westminster Abbey gives Oct. 25th, 1400, as the date of his death and there seems no reason to impugn its accuracy; the monument itself was not erected till the 16th century but the fact remains that, after the date it gives, we hear nothing further of Chaucer.

It can be seen that there is much in the above record which is left vague. We do not, for example, know anything of Chaucer's family. His treatise on the

---

[1] S. Moore, *Anglia*, xxv. (New Series).

Astrolabe is addressed to a ' little son Lewis ' but nothing more is heard of Lewis.

A certain Thomas Chaucer, a wealthy individual who played a prominent part in the next three reigns, those of Henry IV, V, and VI, was, according to tradition, the son of the poet, and there are several small pieces of evidence which seem to connect the two.

Of the poet's personality we have little knowledge, except what can be derived from his own writing. We have one good portrait which we owe to his disciple Occleve ; it represents Chaucer, apparently in old age, and shows a face delicate and refined, almost wistful.

He himself has given us a humorous description of his personal appearance ; in the *Prologue to Sir Thopas* the host addresses him as follows :

> ' what man artow ? quod he ;
> Thou lokest as thou woldest find an hare,
> For ever up-on the ground I see thee stare.
> Now war you, sirs, and lat this man have place ;
> He in the waast is shape as wel as I ;
>   smal and fair of face.
> He semeth elvish by his contenaunce
> For unto no wight dooth he daliaunce.'

Chaucer's references to his own tastes and habits are few and the most important occur in the *Hous of Fame* and the *Prologue to the Legend of Good Women*. In the former the eagle twits him with his intense devotion to study ; after his labours in the counting-house he goes home and stupefies himself with another book :

> ' For whan thy labour doon al is,
> And hast y-maad thy rekeninges,
> In stede of rest and newe thinges,
> Thou goest hoom to thy house anoon ;
> And, also doumb as any stoon,
> Thou sittest at another boke,
> Till fully daswed is thy loke.'

In the same passage the eagle observes that the poet is so completely absorbed in his own concerns that he hears nothing, even of his neighbours, and would live exactly like a hermit were it not for the fact that his abstinence is but little[1].

In the *Legend of Good Women* (the Prologue) he tells us that he holds books in very great reverence, he loves to read in them and nothing will draw him away except occasionally upon a holiday or when the month of May arrives.

> 'Whan that I here the smale foules singe,
> And that the floures ginne for to springe,
> Farwel my studie, as lasting that sesoun.'

Chaucer had, evidently, a great love of nature though, as is the case with most mediaeval poets, he limited his interest mainly to one season—the spring; of this there are many wonderful descriptions in the *Prologue*, the *Knight's Tale*, etc., etc.

The facts of Chaucer's life show us that he was, during by far the greater part, actively engaged in affairs and, under the circumstances, it must have needed an amazing amount of industry to leave so large a volume of work. It is not surprising that Chaucer is a poet of ' torsos ' and that quite a number of his poems, including some of the very best—*The Legend of Good Women*, *The Squire's Tale*, etc., etc. were left unfinished. There were occasions when he felt the double burden a very heavy one, and the *Hous of Fame* seems to have been written, in part at least, as an entreaty for relief.

Chaucer's continual contact with life helps to explain, no doubt, the reality of his work. Few poets can have known the world more widely.

He was acquainted with kings and princes, probably, in the case of John of Gaunt at least, quite intimately. He treats of great nobles with the humour which marks familiarity : thus his Theseus, in his despotism, his fits of anger, his willingness to be ' assuaged ' by the ladies of his family, especially when they go on their knees to

[1] *Hous of Fame* 640—660.

entreat mercy for captives, his stately hospitality, his
love of lovers and his love of chivalry—Theseus, in all
this, is very like a Plantagenet prince and has, notwithstanding his mythical surroundings, a vivid truth.

Chaucer's offices of Comptroller and Clerk of the
Works must have brought him in contact, equally well,
with the middle class, and his journeys abroad both
widened his mind and taught him to see his own country
more clearly, freshly and distinctly.

Chaucer has provided the reader with several lists of
his works. In the Prologue to the *Legend* the god of love
accuses Chaucer of having written poems which tend to
disgust men with love such as the *Romance of the Rose* :

'That is an heresye ageyns my lawe' ;

and also complains of *Troilus and Criseyde*. Alcestis,
on the other hand, quotes many works which tend,
either directly or indirectly, to the honour of women :
the *Hous of Fame, The Deeth of Blaunche the Duchesse,
The Parlement of Foules*, etc., etc. There is another
list in the prologue to the *Man of Law's Tale* which deals
mainly with *The Legend of Good Women* and its contents,
though they do not tally with the poem as we possess it,
and seem to show that Chaucer had contemplated an
extension.

There is again a third list in a retractation appended
to the *Canterbury Tales* in which the author expresses
contrition for such of those tales as 'sounen[1] unto sinne'
but claims credit for the rest. Lydgate in the prologue
to his *Falls of Princes* also gives a list of Chaucer's works.

From these four taken together a very reliable canon
may be compiled though it is evident that some works
have disappeared such as the one which Chaucer calls
The Book of the Lion or the one Lydgate terms *Daunt in
Englyssh* which may, very possibly, have consisted of
translations from Dante like the life of Ugo in the

[1] Tend.

Monk's Tale. Some short pieces are also ascribed to Chaucer on very reliable MS. evidence.

Chaucer tells us that he translated *The Romance of the Rose*[1], but the existing translation, traditionally ascribed to him, is both incomplete and inconsecutive; it falls into three distinct portions and differences of dialect and of technique suggest that the three may be by different authors; it is possible that only the first portion is Chaucer's. This is one of the most charming, sweet and gay of all Middle English poems, full of admirable pictures. Its delicate and refined portraits of women—allegorical figures—greatly influenced Spenser. We may quote a few lines to show how close their manner is to that of *The Faerie Queene*. Chaucer says of Ydelnesse:

> ' Hir face whyt and wel coloured,
> With litel mouth and round to see;
> A clove chin eek hadde she.
>
> .   .   .   .   .   .
> Hir throte also whyt of hewe
> As snow on braunche snowed newe.'

And of Fraunchyse:

> ' With eyen gladde, and browes bente;
> Hir heer doun to hir heles wente.
> And she was simple as douve on tree,
> Ful debonaire of herte was she.'

There are also many striking single lines such as the description of Poverty:

> ' For naked as a worm was she.'

In the Prologue to the *Legend* Alcestis mentions the poet as having composed many songs in honour of the god of love:

> ' And many an ympne for your halydayes,
> That highten Balades, Roundels, Virelayes.'

The works referred to were, in all probability, lyrical poems in the French fashion and the greater number must have perished as comparatively few survive; some of

---

[1] *Prologue to Legend.*

these such as *Merciles Beaute, a Triple Roundel, To Rose-mounde, a Balade* are little more than metrical exercises.

On the other hand some of the later ' balades ' whose subjects were taken from Boethius are nobly beautiful, and we have at least one exquisite specimen of the love ' balade '—that contained in the Prologue to the *Legend* :

> ' Hyd, Absolon, thy gilte tresses clere ;
> Ester, ley thou thy meknesse al adoun.
> ...Hyde ye your beauties, Isoude and Eleyne,
> My lady cometh, that al this may disteyne.'

This poem anticipates Villon's ' balade ' on the ' Dames du temps jadis ' though it has not the same intensity of haunting pathos.

If many of Chaucer's lost songs equalled these later ones then the disappearance of his lyrical work must be regarded as one of the greatest misfortunes of English letters.

Chaucer's earliest original poem of any length appears to have been the *Book of the Duchesse* dated by its subject 1369. Here, though we find the poet essaying his strength, he only ventures upon brief flights, for he is still largely imitative ; the poem is in fact almost a ' cento ' compiled from different authors, such as the two poets of the *Roman de la Rose*, de Lorris and de Meung, Guillaume de Machault, etc., etc. The best thing it contains is the portrait of the Duchess herself whom Chaucer probably knew ; even this is somewhat conventionalised but it remains a noble expression of the mediaeval ideal. It is the veritable portrait of a great lady, free from all envy, speaking no evil, full of sweet courtesy, loyal in all her deeds and, above everything, true and true and yet again true :

> ' And I dar seyn and swere hit wel—
> That Trouthe him-self, over al and al,
> Had chose his maner principal
> In hir, that was his resting-place[1].'

[1] ll. 1002–5.

Here again we have an anticipation of Spenser whose Una and Amoret are essentially of the same type as Chaucer's ' gode faire Whyte ' (*i.e.* Blanche).

The period of Chaucer's life, from 1372 to 1386, is often spoken of as the ' Italian ' period because in it Italian influence predominates though it is worthy of note that the French influence never wholly disappears.

Chaucer's metre, in his earliest poems, is the octo-syllabic couplet ; after 1372 his favourite metre becomes the seven-lined stanza. Mr Saintsbury remarks that ' his pitching on it and his preference for it are fresh proofs of his instinctive genius for prosody[1].'

Chaucer experiments very beautifully with this metre in the *Parlement of Foules* and brings it to perfection in *Troilus and Criseyde*.

It is the custom to assign a certain number of the *Canterbury Tales*, the majority of those written in stanza, to this period : the *Second Nun's Tale* of St Cecilia ; the *Man of Law's Tale*—the story of Constance—the unhappy royal heroine who floats for ' years and days ' upon the sea, all alone in a small boat without food or drink but sustained by divine power. Both these are obviously early work for they are very naïve and primitive. The *Clerk's* story of Griseldis may also belong to this period though, possibly, it was re-written for the *Canterbury Tales* ; it is, at any rate, one of the most exquisite things that Chaucer has wrought, all pathos and tenderness ; the portrait of Griseldis, though in a wholly different kind, is as noble as that of the Duchesse and she is made to live and move before our eyes. To this period there certainly belongs some version of the *Knight's Tale*, for in the *Prologue to the Legend* Chaucer speaks of having written a work entitled *Al the love of Palamon and Arcite* ; it is possible that the poem he alludes to is not the one we possess but an earlier version in stanza.

[1] *History of Prosody.*

The independent works of this second period are the *Parlement of Foules, Troilus and Criseyde* and the *Hous of Fame*.

The first of these is dated by its subject 1382 ; it is a court piece, written to celebrate a royal betrothal, almost certainly that of Richard II to Anne of Bohemia, for all the circumstances tally. It is Chaucer's welcome to the gracious lady who was to become his queen and patroness.

There are reminiscences of the *Roman de la Rose*, of Boccaccio and Dante. It is a dream-allegory, relating how the birds meet on St Valentine's day to choose their mates and how the eagles, who represent the royal lovers, receive the precedence. The chief fascination of the poem lies in the delicacy of its courtly compliment and its naïve and quiet humour. As we shall see later, it anticipates in some ways the subject of the *Nonnë Prestes Tale*.

Troilus and Criseyde probably dates from 1382 or later[1]. It is a very long poem and, the *Canterbury Tales* apart, Chaucer's most ambitious effort. It is founded on the *Filostrato* of Boccaccio, though the story was already well known before it reached his hands, was, in fact, one of the world's great love-tales. Chaucer takes the Italian poem mainly as a theme upon which to embroider and invents about two-thirds of his total result. He has very greatly changed the characters, making both hero and heroine more attractive, and he has re-created the character of Pandarus. The scene is laid in the Homeric age but, without the slightest consciousness of anachronism, Chaucer has employed throughout the manners and customs of the Middle Ages. The poem has its faults—it contains far too many digressions—but it embodies the very heart and soul of romance and its psychology of love is subtle and true. It is, for passion

[1] There is an undoubted reference to Anne of Bohemia I. 25.

and sweetness, Chaucer's *Romeo and Juliet*. It contains also Chaucer's Falstaff, for Pandarus is one of the great comic creations of English letters, the whole portrait abounds in humour and, as is the case with Falstaff, the poet has reconciled us to what are, seemingly, the most unattractive traits.

It is full of richest poetry :

> ' And white thinges wexen dimme and donne
> For lak of light, and sterres for to appere[1].'

> ' A nightingale, upon a cedre grene,
> Under the chambre-wal ther as she lay,
> Ful loude sang ayein the mone shene,
> Paraunter, in his briddes wyse, a lay
> Of love, that made hir herte fresh and gay[2].'

The poem is Chaucer's most perfect specimen of a romance ; he attempted the same type of subject again in the *Knight's Tale* but, beautiful as that work is, its love-story is slight and conventional when compared with the passion of Troilus.

The *Hous of Fame* is usually dated about 1384. It returns to the octosyllabic couplet and the dream-allegory ; it seems to have been composed either hastily or somewhat carelessly, for it is not well conceived as a whole and was left incomplete. Chaucer shows his great admiration for Virgil by introducing, somewhat inappropriately, a brief epitome of the *Aeneid*. The main substance of the poem is a reflection on earthly fame, its transitory nature, its uncertainty, the injustice with which it is awarded. Chaucer seems to be asking himself if the poetic craft were really worth the labour and the toil ; perhaps he was exhausted by the long effort of *Troilus*. The poem is, however, one of the best examples of that ' elvish ' humour which was so marked a feature in his personality ; nothing could be more perfect in its kind than the dialogue between the

[1] ll. 130.　　　　　　　　[2] ll. 132.

poet and the golden eagle who conveys him through the air to the house of Fame and offers on the way to teach him astronomy since they are in such an unrivalled position for observing the stars. Here again we may notice in the learned seriousness of the bird a certain anticipation of the *Nonně Prestes Tale*.

The *Legend of Good Women* (usually dated 1386) is the first of Chaucer's poems composed in the ten-syllabled or heroic couplet ; this had for some time been one of the favourite metres of French poetry and Chaucer, by his masterly employment of it, made it one of the standard metres for English also.

The *Legend*, as we have said, is plainly intended as a compliment to the queen in return for some service. In the prologue Anne of Bohemia, in the allegorical disguise of Alcestis, defends the poet against the attacks of Cupid, and the poet promises to make amends for his slanders upon women by narrating the lives of women who have been martyrs to love or as he says elsewhere the 'Seintes Legendes of Cupyde[1].' Chaucer gives a fascinating portrait of the queen, who is another of his really noble types of womanhood ; it was, indeed, exceedingly appropriate to compare her to Alcestis, for Anne of Bohemia was veritably the good angel of her husband and had she survived longer the issue of his life and his reign might have been far more fortunate.

The heroines treated of in the *Legend* are all classical, selected very largely from Ovid. They are rather curiously chosen, for some of them, such as Cleopatra and Medea, can hardly be regarded as 'seintes' in any sense of the term. Nine stories are told, brief but fine examples of narrative, and then the poem breaks off. Chaucer probably found that the plan was too monotonous and that the stories, with their predestined tragic endings, were becoming, in the mass, too sombre.

[1] *Man of Law's Prologue.*

He laid it aside for a work which permitted of more variety and provided full scope for his humour.

The *Canterbury Tales* are Chaucer's greatest achievement because they embody his most mature and varied work. In them he reveals himself emphatically and beyond question the greatest narrative poet in the English language and, indeed, one of the great narrative poets of the world. He has gained the perfect knowledge of all that makes a good story—not too long, continually reminding both himself and the reader that prolixity destroys interest ; on the other hand he is not too brief ; he allows himself sufficient room for humorous dialogue, sufficient space to develop character and at times, as in the *Knight's Tale*, for really gorgeous description. The tales themselves are excellent, but the links between are better still ; these links are really a continuation of the general Prologue ; they show the best comic dialogue which we possess before the time of Shakespeare and suggest that, in a different age, Chaucer might have made a dramatist of the rarest kind.

His power of character-drawing is revealed at its best in his masterpiece—the general Prologue. We have commented before on the wealth and variety of the types displayed but we may observe further the peculiar method by which the character is presented. Chaucer's description is mainly of externalities but each detail is so chosen that the effect is not external at all, the poet gets to the heart and lays bare the very springs of conduct or suggests the whole manner of life.

Thus the Reve rides ever ' the hindreste of our route,' and this is characteristic of the man, for he is accustomed to watch everyone and spy upon everyone ; the Knight rides in doublet of fustian stained with the marks of his armour which reveals at once his simple and unpretentious nature ; the ' brown visage ' of the Yeoman suggests his open air life and the sheaf of ' pecok arwes ' all the merriment of Merrie England. The minutest touch tells ;

that art of selection which signalises the master in every craft has never been carried to greater perfection than here.

The *Canterbury Tales* are not quite continuous ; the links between break here and there so that the tales themselves fall into groups which critics designate as A, B, C, etc.

Chaucer is careful to vary the tales within the same group so that he passes from romantic to humorous, refined to broad, etc. The tales are, as a rule, excellently adapted to the character of the narrator, but they might also be divided according to subject-matter, *i.e.* romantic tales, fabliaux or tales of popular life, fables proper, saint legends, etc.

The romantic group include the *Knight's Tale*, the *Squire's*, the *Franklin's*, etc. The *Knight's Tale* leads off and is the most ambitious of the whole series ; it is adapted from Boccaccio's epic poem—the *Teseide*— which Chaucer considerably abbreviates. It is a noble poem, abounding in the richest poetry, pure and exalted in its tone and temper ; its defect lies in a certain conventionality of character ; Theseus is really the most outstanding figure though he is shown only for a brief space, but the two heroes themselves are hardly living types. Those portions of the poem which linger in the memory are the descriptions which, in their own way, have never been surpassed : the description of the heroine Emily, of the May morning in the forest when the ' bisy larke ' begins to sing and

' Al the Orient laugheth of the light,'

the description of the three temples, the two gorgeous portraits of Lygurge the king of Thrace and Emetreus the king of Inde, portraits that glow with manly beauty and with manly power and that give the very essence and soul of chivalry. The account of the tournament is also most vivid ; Chaucer had probably been an eyewitness of what he describes ; it is very like the descriptions of tournaments which we meet in the pages of Froissart but with the added vitality of poetry.

The *Squire's Tale* is a story of Eastern magic ; it ends abruptly, but, even as it stands, it is one of the most fascinating of Chaucer's works and would, if completed, have been a fitting pendant to the *Knight's Tale* ; here, centuries before Coleridge, Chaucer has anticipated his secret of making the supernatural seem plausible by the truth of the feelings and sensations with which it is associated. The poem has been estimated, whether rightly or not, to have been intended ultimately as a piece of court-compliment.

The group of saint-legends include a good deal of early and rather inferior work such as the *Second Nun's Tale* and the *Man of Law's Tale* already alluded to, but one story—the *Prioress's Tale*—is among the gems of Chaucer's collection. The tale is the familiar one of the Christian boy murdered by Jews, but it is marvellously told ; the ' litel clergeon, seven yeer of age,' has all the pure joy of childhood and Chaucer has nowhere shown more sweetness and tenderness. The murder of a child might seem a subject almost too horrible for art, but the real stress is not laid on the crime but, as it should be, on the miracle by which the Virgin consoles the child and bids him sing, even in death, his triumphant hymn of ' Alma Redemptoris mater.' The perfect reverence of the narrative is a notable point ; here Chaucer who so often has ' the accent ' of the Renaissance and the Reformation, ironical, sceptical, critical, Chaucer for once catches the genuine tone of the Middle Ages and their naïve unquestioning faith.

The so-called ' Fabliaux ' form a group with absolutely different qualities. They are tales of contemporary life, dealing with the lower middle-class—millers, carpenters, etc.—and are related with the utmost possible realism. They are all coarse, like Boccaccio or even like

Rabelais, but the humour is splendid and every detail vivid ; the general atmosphere is what the narrators themselves would call ' jolly ' and they give us the most vivid picture we possess of the England of that day with its quaint peculiarities of dress and custom ; a masterly portrait, for example, is that of ' Absolon ' the parish clerk, whose yellow hair is elaborately curled, and stands out ' as broad as a fan,' parted with exact and precise neatness down the middle ; he has the most ornate shoes and red stockings ; his ' kirtel ' is of light blue and he wears a surplice as white as the flower of the rye. Absolon is accomplished in dancing country dances, ' casting his legs to and fro,' in singing and playing on a small ' rubible ' (*i.e.* fiddle). Also he thinks himself irresistible. From the purely literary point of view Chaucer's ' fabliaux ' are among his best works though their coarseness has prevented them from being generally known. Of the fable proper there are three examples, two of the beast fable—the *Nonnë Prestes Tale* and the *Manciple's*—and one moral fable—the *Pardoner's Tale*. The latter is the most grimly impressive thing which Chaucer ever penned. The scene is laid in ' Flandres ' in a time of pestilence which is described briefly but with the sombre realism of one who had seen it with his own eyes ; three ' rioters,' beside themselves with reck-lessness and arrogance, insolently determine to go in search of the rascal ' Death ' who is slaying so many ; they are directed to him by an old man who tells them they will find him under a certain tree ; they discover there a great heap of gold which does indeed, by their mutual treachery and murder, bring about the destruc-tion of all three. The sombre power of the narrative is in startling contrast to the cynical humour of the Par-doner's own prologue.

A curious group is formed by the mediaeval prose sermons of which there are two specimens—the tale of *Melibeus* (told by Chaucer himself) and the *Persoun's Tale*;

these are good examples of 14th century prose but there is nothing either original or interesting in their subjects.

There are also a number of miscellaneous narratives, such as the *Chanoun's Yeoman's Tale*—a brilliant exposure of alchemy, and *Sir Thopas* (Chaucer's own)—a clever burlesque of the rhymed romances.

Every reader of Chaucer must be impressed by the combination in him of what might seem the most opposite qualities ; on the one side he is abstract, ideal and chivalrous, beautiful as Spenser himself. On the other he is as absolutely true to life and as coarsely realistic as Fielding.

Like Shakespeare, who paints with equal facility Titania and Justice Shallow, Rosalind and Ancient Pistol, Chaucer draws with equal zest the portraits of ' Emetreus of Inde ' and of ' Absolon ' the parish clerk— the incarnate essence of chivalry and the incarnate essence of pretentious absurdity.

With the same impartiality he shows us the sentimentality of the prioress, crying if a dog is so much as scolded, and her purity and tenderness of heart.

Chaucer cannot rival Shakespeare in heights and depths, but he certainly does in breadth and impartiality of mind. He is the greatest of all English narrative poets and unsurpassed as a humourist and satirist.

II

Chronological Tables

A

CHAUCER'S LIFE

1340. Birth of Geoffrey Chaucer. This date is uncertain.

1357. In the household accounts of Elizabeth, Duchess of Clarence, mention is made of clothes and other articles purchased for ' Geoffrey Chaucer ' who has the standing of a page.

1359. Chaucer joins the military expedition to France and is made prisoner.

1360. Chaucer is ransomed from imprisonment, Edward III contributing towards his ransom £16. The war ends with the treaty of Bretigny.

1366. A pension is granted to a certain 'Philippa Chaucer,' one of the queen's ladies, which pension is afterwards paid through her husband Geoffrey Chaucer.

1367. A pension is granted to Chaucer as one of the valets of the king's household.

1369. Blanche, the first wife of John of Gaunt, dies at the age of twenty-nine; Chaucer writes in her honour the poem entitled *The Dethe of Blaunche the Duchesse* or *The Book of the Duchesse*.

1372. Chaucer, acting with two others, is sent on a mission to Genoa concerning trade. He remained in Italy for nearly a year and probably met Petrarch at Padua.

1374. Chaucer is granted a pitcher of wine daily to be received from the king's butler, a gift afterwards commuted for a yearly pension of 20 marks.

On June 8th he is appointed Comptroller of the Customs in Wool, Skins and Leather for the port of London.

A few days later he and his wife Philippa receive a pension of £10 a year for life in recompense for services rendered by them.

1377. Chaucer is sent on important missions to Flanders and to France.

In June Edward III dies and is succeeded by his grandson Richard II.

1378. Chaucer, in company with three knights, is sent on a mission to France to negotiate for the marriage of Richard II to 'a daughter of France'; the project comes to nothing.

In the same year he accompanies Sir Edward Berkeley to Italy on a mission to Bernabo Visconti, tyrant of

Milan. He appoints the poet Gower as one of his agents to represent him during his absence.

1381. The pension of Geoffrey Chaucer and his wife Philippa is confirmed by Richard II.

1382. Richard II marries Anne of Bohemia. Chaucer is appointed Comptroller of the Petty Customs in addition to his former office but is permitted to exercise the functions of the new post by deputy.

1384. He is allowed a deputy for his former office—as Comptroller of the Wool Quay at London, and is probably indebted to the queen for this favour.

1386. Chaucer is elected Knight of the Shire for Kent. The Parliament of this year compels the king to grant a patent by which he is deprived of power and the supreme authority falls into the hands of Gloucester.

Chaucer loses his two Comptrollerships and is reduced to raising money on his pensions. In October occurs the Scrope and Grosvenor trial in which Chaucer is described as XL ans et plus and is said to have borne arms for twenty-seven years.

1387. The death of Philippa Chaucer.

1389. Richard II takes the government into his own hands and John of Gaunt returns to England. The Lancastrian party is again in power and Chaucer receives the appointment of Clerk of the King's Works at the palace of Westminster, the Tower of London, etc.

1390. Chaucer is appointed on a Commission with five others to repair the banks of the Thames between Woolwich and Greenwich.

He is also appointed joint Forester (with Richard Brittle) of North Petherton Park in Somerset.

1391. Chaucer loses his appointment as 'Clerk of the Works.'

1394. Chaucer receives a grant from the king of £20 a year for life.

1395. Chaucer is in pecuniary difficulties and raises money in advance on his pensions.

1398. Chaucer is still in difficulties and the king grants him letters of protection against creditors.

1399. Henry of Lancaster is declared king on Sept. 30th. Chaucer addresses to him a poem entitled ' Compleynt to his Empty Purse ' and the king doubles his pension.

1400. Chaucer dies ; the date given upon his tombstone is Oct. 25th, 1400.

B

CHAUCER'S WORKS

FIRST PERIOD   —1369

The A B C: a poem so called because each stanza begins with a different letter of the alphabet : it is a hymn to the Virgin paraphrased from a French poet—Guillaume de Deguileville.

The Compleynt to Pite : a brief and artificial love-poem.

The Romaunt of the Rose : a translation from the French *Roman de la Rose* by the two poets Guillaume de Lorris and Jean de Meung. The first part is a love-allegory, the second resolves itself into a satire upon women and upon the clergy.

The Dethe of Blaunche the Duchesse or *the Book of the Duchesse :* a poem suggested by the death of Blanche of Lancaster, dated 1369 by its subject. A portion of this (ll. 62—222) probably represents an earlier poem—the *Ceys and Alcione* mentioned in the head-link to the *Man of Law's Tale*.

The Lyf of Saint Cecyle : probably but not certainly of this period. Afterwards made the *Second Nun's Tale*.

The Monk's Tale : a series of tragedies dealing with the lives of great men, beginning with Lucifer and Adam and coming down to Chaucer's own contemporaries. Four of these lives were probably added later as that of Bernabo Visconti cannot possibly be early.

Lyrical Poems. Chaucer says that he wrote a large number of ' balades, roundels, virelayes ' most of which appear to have been lost.

SECOND PERIOD 1369—1386

The Man of Law's Tale : a saint-legend based upon the Anglo-Norman Chronicle of Nicholas Trivet.

The Clerk's Tale. This cannot be earlier than 1373 as it is founded on Petrarch's Latin version of the story of Griseldis which was made in that year.

Palamon and Arcite : a poem either identical with the *Knight's Tale* or on the same subject, possibly in seven-lined stanza.

Compleynte to his Lady : a brief love-poem.

Anelida and Arcite : a short incomplete love-poem, containing several stanzas translated from the *Teseide.*

The Tale of Melibeus. Partly translated from Alber-tano of Brescia and included in the *Canterbury Tales* as the second one chosen by Chaucer.

The Parlement of Foules : an allegorical poem to celebrate a royal betrothal, probably that of Richard II to Anne of Bohemia : dated 1382 by its subject.

The Persoun's Tale : a mediaeval sermon.

Troilus and Criseyde : adapted from Boccaccio's *Il Filostrato* with a few stanzas from the *Teseide.* Dated 1382 or later by a reference to Anne of Bohemia.

Boethius : a translation of the ' De Consolatione Philosophiae ' ; its author Boethius, the most learned philosopher of his time, was born at Rome about A.D. 480 and put to death by the emperor Theodoric the Goth in A.D. 524.

There are so many references to this work in *Troilus and Criseyde* that Chaucer was probably intent upon both about the same time.

The Hous of Fame : probably written about 1383 or 4 ; it seems to be a lament by Chaucer over the burdensome nature of his official duties.

LAST PERIOD 1386—1400

The Legend of Good Women : This must be dated later than the preceding works since it mentions the most important among them. It is dedicated to the queen in an allegorical prologue and breaks off after nine tales.

The Canterbury Tales : These do not form one continuous group, for the links connecting them fail in places. From the references to time it is evident that they are supposed to be told on four different days. The total work is only about a quarter of the original plan : Chaucer had intended that each pilgrim should tell four tales, two on the outward journey and two on the homeward (Prologue 791–5), but in the actual form no pilgrim tells more than one except Chaucer himself and he only because his first tale—*Sir Thopas*—is interrupted by the host. No member of the group of mechanics tells a tale nor does the yeoman, though the tale of Gamelyn, which is the same story as that of *As You Like It*, is included in some mss. as his ; it would have been a very suitable subject for the Yeoman and probably represents rough material which Chaucer intended to work up. Two unexpected pilgrims—a Canon and his Yeoman—join on the route, and the Yeoman tells a tale which exposes his master's practices in alchemy.

C

ORDER OF THE CANTERBURY TALES

GROUP A.

General Prologue. Knight's Tale. Miller's Tale. Reeve's Tale. Cook's Tale.

GROUP B.

Man of Law's Tale. Shipman's Tale. Prioress's Tale. Tale of Sir Thopas (Chaucer). *Tale of Melibeus* (Chaucer). *Monk's Tale. Nonnë Prestes Tale.*

GROUP C.

Physician's Tale. Pardoner's Tale.

GROUP D.

Wife of Bath's Tale. Friar's Tale. Summoner's Tale.

GROUP E.

Clerk's Tale. Merchant's Tale.

GROUP F.

Squire's Tale. Franklin's Tale.

GROUP G.

Second Nun's Tale. Canon's Yeoman's Tale.

GROUP H.

Manciple's Tale.

GROUP I.

Parsoun's Tale.

According to the notes of place and time mentioned on the way Group A seems to have been intended for relation on the first day, Group B on the second day, Groups C, D and E on the third day and the remainder on the fourth.

The Nonnë Prestes Tale would thus be the last narrated on the second day.

III

(*a*). SOURCES OF THE NONNË PRESTES TALE

The *Nonnë Prestes Tale*—the story of the cock and the fox—belongs to the group of popular fables known as the *Roman de Renart*. The *Roman de Renart* grew up, by degrees, out of a number of animal tales.

Beast-fables, of one type or another, are spread all over Europe ; many of them come from the east ; nearly all those tales which have the lion as their hero appear to be of eastern origin but the majority of the fables, as they travelled north, gradually substituted northern animals. Thus, instead of the lion, the hyaena and the jackal, we have, in the European versions, the bear, the fox and the wolf.

The fables of Aesop are among the best and earliest examples of these folk tales to acquire literary currency and become embodied in a permanent form. The *Roman de Renart*, however, branched off in a different direction; its fables are much less serious than those of Aesop and differ also because they are united together to form a kind of animal epic whose hero is the fox. The *Roman de Renart* reveals its popular origin by the fact that the sympathy of the authors goes mainly with the weak; the fox is continually in conflict with animals far stronger than himself—the wolf, the bear, the stag—and he conquers them all by his cunning and cleverness; it is in accord also with the general spirit of the epic that, when the fox has to deal with creatures who are weaker than he—the cock, the tomtit, the crow and the sparrow—he nearly always gets the worst of it, indeed in the older versions the fox is invariably defeated when he comes into conflict with a bird, and the tales dealing with birds thus form a special group by themselves in which the fox is always outwitted and overcome.

The *Roman de Renart* grew up in different countries about the same time. One of the earliest versions known—the *Reinhart Fuchs* of Henri de Glichezare, was translated from the French by an Alsatian and dates about 1180. The main bulk of the French *Roman de Renart* exists in MSS. of the thirteenth and fourteenth centuries; there are also numerous German versions and the earliest *printed* version in English (Caxton's) is translated from the Dutch.

The names employed in the *Roman de Renart* are partly of French, partly of German origin. Those which typify the characters of the animals such as Chantecler the cock, Noble the lion and Fière the lioness are, usually, later than the rest. Many of the names—Renart, Isengrin (the wolf), Tibert (the cat)—are of Germanic origin.

We may notice in this connection that the name Chaucer gives his cock 'Chantecler' is the name of the *Roman de Renart* ; the name of Chaucer's fox ' Russell ' is also to be found in the *Roman* where he is represented as the son of Renart ; it was probably chosen by Chaucer because it was a common term for a fox in England—russell meaning ' the red.'

The *Roman de Renart* forms an admirable collection of fables ; many of the stories are really fine specimens of narrative art, full of witty and attractive dialogue, with the characters well developed and defined. The habits of the animals are described with great realism ; their appearance, their movements, the cries they make—are all true to life. Chantecler is depicted perching on a roof :

> ' L'un ueil ouvert et l'autre clos,
> L'un pié crampi et l'autre droit '

(one eye open and one closed, one foot drawn up and the other straight) or he is described as strutting proudly before his hens, stretching out his neck, ' tendant le col.'

It is worthy of note that Chaucer also employs a similar realism and studies his hero with accuracy and humour :

> ' He loketh as it were a grym leoun,
> And on his toos he rometh up and down,
> Him deigned not to sette his foot to grounde,
> He chukketh when he hath a corn y-founde
> And to him rennen thanne his wyves alle ! '

The *Roman de Renart* is also full of gaiety and good-humour. In the later versions the element of satire becomes larger and more prominent and the authors especially take pleasure in satirising pedantry by representing the animals as skilled in all the resources of mediaeval learning. Thus in *Renard le Contrefait* (composed at Troyes in the first quarter of the fourteenth century) the fox argues in the most eloquent manner ; he discusses theology and metaphysics, astronomy and astrology, he is well skilled in mediaeval medicine, he quotes history and mythology. When Chantecler comes to Noble to complain of the massacre of his family who have been slain by Renard he compares his own lamentable loss to the miseries of Troy when it was overthrown. When he has himself just escaped from Renard the two converse together and quote learned authors on either side—Cato, Cicero, Seneca, Saint Augustine.

Chaucer gives us in the *Nonnë Prestes Tale* an excellent adaptation of this ' motive.' His cock is skilled in astronomy for he can crow exactly at the correct hours !

> ' By nature knew he ech ascencioun
> Of equinoxial in thilke toun.'

The hen is an authority on mediaeval medicine ; she knows all about ' complexions ' and ' humours,' the difference between ' red choleric ' humour and melancholy ; she can recommend a whole list of herbs and she refers her husband to Cato as an author who put no trust in dreams. The cock, in his reply, quotes Cicero and Macrobius, and the fox when he flatters the cock refers to Boethius, etc. When the fox is carried away the lamentation is as great as at the destruction of Troy, etc.

The outline of his story in its incidents Chaucer has drawn from the *Roman de Renart* proper, but his general method much more closely resembles *Renard le Contrefait* and it seems extremely probable that he knew that version too.

It has been already remarked that the adventures with birds form a quite distinctive group in the *Roman de Renart* for the reason that the fox is almost invariably outwitted. Glichezare has three episodes in which the fox is tricked successively by the cock, the tomtit and the crow, and other episodes are added in later versions.

The history of Chaucer's special story is rather a long one and can be traced before it reaches the Renart cycle.

A well-known fable of Aesop—the dog and the cock—includes in germ most of the Chantecler motives.

It runs as follows : a dog and a cock are travelling together when they are overtaken by night. The cock perches upon a tree and the dog lies down in the hollow beneath. At his accustomed hour the cock crows. The fox hears him, comes up and entices him to descend ; he says that he wishes to embrace the creature possessed of such a beautiful voice. The cock assents but says : 'First waken the porter ; he is sleeping at the foot of the tree.' The fox arouses the dog who leaps upon him and tears him in pieces. In this story three different motives can be traced : the crowing of the cock on the tree, the fox's flattery and the attack of the dog.

In this fable (of Greek origin) the dog is the companion of the cock, but in all the French versions the single dog is replaced by several and their part in the story is quite different ; they enter only because the tale ends with a pursuit by men and dogs.

By degrees the story was improved upon and grew more detailed : the cock allows himself to be duped by the flattery of the fox, becomes momentarily his victim but, in his turn, dupes the fox and escapes.

In Henri de Glichezare's version the tale runs : Reinhart has penetrated into the yard of master Lanzelin and lies down near Schanteclêr. The latter is asleep and dreaming ; he is aroused by the outcries of his hen Pinte and her companions who take to flight when they perceive the fox. Schanteclêr reassures them and narrates his dream Pinte, in reply, tells him of the strange animal she has seen—the fox—and entreats him not, through his rashness, to leave her and her children orphans ; she persuades him to mount on a thorn-bush. Reinhart comes to the foot of the bush, praises Schantecl êr's beautiful voice and flatters him till he descends. Reinhart then seizes the cock and carries him off, but he is pursued by the peasants who shout out execrations ; he opens his mouth to reply and Schanteclêr escapes.

In this version there are several additions to the story : there is the introduction of the cock's dream which he narrates to his wife—Pinte ; we have the conversation between the hen and the cock, discussing the dream ; again the fox's flattery is successful and he does prevail and does seize the cock, only in replying to the insults of the peasants he lets him go.

In the later French versions—the *Roman de Renart* proper—we have still further details and it appears to have been this which was the source directly employed by Chaucer.

Its narrative runs as follows : Renart, by means of a gap in the hedge, penetrates into the courtyard of a certain farmer, Constant de Noes. At the noise he makes Pinte and her chickens flee in alarm ; Chantecler laughs at their terror and stations himself upon a roof. He goes to sleep and dreams :

> ' Qui li venoit enmi le vis,
> Et tenoit un ros peliçon
> Dont les goles estoient d'os
> Si li metoit par force el dos[1].'

He wakens trembling with fright and narrates his dream to Pinte. She explains that the creature ' au ros peliçon ' is the fox at present lurking among the cabbages, ready to devour him, and that his dream prophesies that he will fall a victim. Chantecler, however, still remains rash and rebukes the hen for her folly in thinking that he could ever be surprised or taken by force ; nothing could get the better of him in such a way and he is certain that his dream is not a foreboding of any harm :

[1] *Roman de Renart*, v. 137 (ed. Martin).

' Pinte, fait-il, molt par es fole.
Molt as dit vileine parole,
Qui diz que je serai sorpris,
Et que la beste est al porpris
Qui par force me conquerra.
*   *   *   *   *   *   *
Ja nel crerai
Que j'aie mal par icest songe[1].'

Chantecler comes to a dunghill and remains there.
Renart approaches gently and tries to seize him but
he is wary. Then Renart begins to entice him ; he
tells him that they ought to be good friends because
they are relatives :

' Car tu es mes cosins germeins.'

He also reminds him of his dear father Chanteclin who
sang better than any other cock :

' Membre te mes de Chanteclin
Ton bon pere qui t'engendra ?
Onques nus cos si ne chanta.'

Chanteclin sang with the most wonderfully sustained
breath because he closed both his eyes and gave his
whole attention to his voice :

' Et molt par avoit longe aleine
Les deus els clos, la vois ot seine.'

Renart again assures him that he is entirely friendly
and that they are the same flesh and blood.

Chantecler thereupon begins to sing but closes one
eye only :

' Puis jeta Chantecler un bret
L'un oil ot clos et l'autre overt.'

This does not satisfy Renart who rebukes him and
tells him Chanteclin sang far better and it was because
he closed both eyes :

' Ce dist Renars n'as fet neent.
Chanteclins chantoit autrement
A uns lons treiz les eilz digniez.'

[1] *Roman de Renart*, v. 261.

Chantecler decides that he will, really and truly, rival his father :

> ' Lors let aler sa meloudie
> Les oilz digniez par grant air.'

Renart immediately seizes him, grasping him by the neck and rejoicing greatly :

> 'Le prent Renars parmi le col.'

Pinte perceives Chantecler carried away and makes a wild outcry, beside herself with grief :

> ' Si se conmence a dementer.'

She cries out that, if she has lost her husband, all the joy of her life has departed and wishes herself dead. The good woman of the poultry yard happens to approach at that moment and calls to the hens but they none of them appear ; she sees what has befallen and sets the hue and cry upon the fox. Constant de Noes is at the head of the pursuit and summons his dogs and men :

> ' Constans apele son mastin,
> Que tuit apelent Mauvoisin,
> Bardol, Travers, Humbaut, Rebors
> Cores apres Renart le ros.'

The men shout insults after the fox ; Chantecler is in the greatest peril but he retains his presence of mind. ' Don't you hear,' he asks Renart, ' how they insult you ? Tell them that you defy them ! '

> ' Quant il dira : " Renars l'enporte "
> Maugrez vostre " ce poes dire." '

Renart who deceives all the world was in his turn deceived.

> ' Renars qui tot le mont decoit,
> Fu decoüs a cele foiz.'

He opens his mouth and the cock escapes and takes refuge in an apple tree from the safe shelter of which he jibes at his foe. Renart replies by cursing the mouth that chatters when it should be silent :

> ' La boce' fait-il ' soit honie,
> Qui s'entremet de noise fere,
> A l'ore qu'ele se doit tere.'

And the cock replies by wishing evil upon him who
winks and closes his eye when he ought to watch :

> ' Qui s'entremet de someller
> A l'ore que il doit veillier.'

This story so closely resembles Chaucer's that we may
consider it as almost certainly his source.

The main outline is in common, and so are a number
of details ; the cock dreams of an animal ' au ros peliçon '
and Chaucer's cock of one ' betwixe yelwe and reed ' ;
the fox lies down amid the cabbages and Chaucer says :
' in a bed of wortes stille he lay ' ; Chaucer's fox, like
Renart, seizes the cock by the throat ' the gargat,' and
Chaucer also like the *Roman* gives the names of the dogs
and men who pursue the fox :

> ' Ran Colle our dogge, and Talbot and Gerland,
> And Malkin, with a distaf in her hand.'

In the curses that the cock and fox each utter upon
their folly Chaucer's lines read like a translation. The
differences are exceedingly noteworthy as a sign of
Chaucer's literary methods and are a very great improve-
ment.

In the *Roman* the cock narrates his dream and the
hen interprets it correctly and so warns him ; Chaucer
has made the hen incredulous and thus introduced an
opportunity for the fascinating discussion on medicine
and on dreams and also provided an opening for the
display of their characters.

Chaucer has omitted the first attempt of the fox to
seize the cock and surely with advantage, for it is im-
probable that the cock, after such a warning, would really
have permitted himself to be enticed ; Chaucer makes his
Chantecler more sensible and more dignified.

Also the fox does not urge relationship with Chantecler ; there is no play about being ' cosins germeins ' or of the same flesh and blood.

We can see how this detail arose in the *Roman de Renart* from the earlier versions which made Renart wish to ' embrace ' Chantecler, but it is, in itself, somewhat fantastic. Chaucer substitutes a claim for family friendship, in itself far more plausible, with the intensely amusing lines :

> ' My lord your fader (god his soule bless !)
> And eek your moder, of hir gentilesse,
> Han in myn hous ybeen, to my gret ese.'

Another possible source that has been suggested is a fable by Marie de France. This is older and briefer than the version of the *Roman de Renart.* It is so short that it may be quoted :

> ' D'un cok recunte, ki estot
> Sur un femer, e si chantot.
> Par de lez li vient un gupilz,
> Si l'apela par muz beaus diz.
> ' Sire ' fet-il ' mut te vei bel ;
> Unc ne vi si gent' oisel.
> Clere voiz as sur tute rien,
> Fors tun pere, que io vi bien :
> Unc oisel meuz ne chanta ;
> Mes il le fist meuz, kar il cluna.'
> ' Si puis ieo fere ' dist le cocs ;
> Les eles bat, les oilz ad clos,
> Chanter quida plus clerement.
> Li gupil saut, e si le prent ;
> Vers la forest od lui s'en va.
> Par mi un champ v il passa,
> Curent apres tut li pastur ;
> Li chiens le huent tut' entur.
> Veit le gupil, ki le coq tient
> Mar le guaina si par eus vient.
> ' Va ' fet li cocs ' si lur escrie,
> Que sui tuens, ne me larras mie.'
> Li gupil volt parler en haut,
> E li cocs de sa buche saut ;
> Sur un haut fust s'est muntez.
> Quant li gupilz s'est reguardez,

Mut par si tient enfantille,
Que li cocs l'ad si enginné.
De mal talent e de dreit ire
La buche cumence a maudire,
Ke parole quant devereit taire.
Li cocs respunt, ' si dei ieo faire,
Maudire l'oil ki volt cluiner,
Quant il deit guarder e guaiter,
Que mal ne vienge a lur seignur.
Ceo funt li fol tut li plusur,
Parolent quant deivent taiser,
Teisent quant il deivent parler.''

(Our story tells of a cock who stood upon a dunghill and crew. A fox came up and addressed him in flattering terms. 'Sir,' said he, ' you are very beautiful; I have never seen such a splendid bird. I have never heard so clear a voice excepting only your father's which was better still and his was best when he closed his eyes.'

' So with me,' said the cock; he beat his wings, closed his eyes and sang most clearly. The fox leaps up, seizes him and bears him towards the wood. As he crosses a field the dogs and shepherds see him and pursue him with a great outcry. The fox still holds the cock though they are hard upon him. ' Cry out,' says the cock, ' that you have me and will not let me go.'

The fox begins to speak and the cock slips from his mouth and mounts on a tree. When the fox perceives him there he knows that he has been tricked and that the cock has the better of him and he curses the mouth that speaks when it should be silent; the cock replies and curses the eye that winks when it should watch and see that no harm comes to its owner. Fools are always doing the wrong thing: they speak when they ought to keep silent and they keep silent when they ought to speak.)

It will be seen that this fable possesses the main outline, nevertheless there are a good many points, very important in the *Roman de Renart* and in Chaucer, which are omitted. There is no mention of Chantecler's pro-

5   w c

phetic dream of the strange animal ; the hen is not mentioned and no discourse with her is possible ; there is no mention of the fox breaking in through the fence ; there is no mention of the wild outcry of the hens ; in fact Marie's fable gives no hint, no starting-point even, for the two things that are most excellent in the Chaucerian version—the prophetic dream and the relations between Chantecler and Partlet.

There is another bird narrative in the *Roman de Renart* which closely resembles the Chantecler story, *i.e.* the tale of Tiecelin the crow. Its outline is as follows : Tiecelin perceives, drying in the sun, a number of small cheeses ; he snatches one, jeers at the old woman who is watching them and flies off with his booty. He perches on the bough of a tree, eating his cheese, and a piece falls down. Renart comes up, flatters him concerning his beautiful voice and so persuades him to drop the cheese. Renart then tries to capture Tiecelin himself but this time the bird outwits him.

This tale is worth mentioning because the figure of the old woman, the dairy-woman, may have suggested Chaucer's old woman who was ' as it were, a maner deye.'

Chaucer's old woman lives in a small cottage :

' Beside a grove, standing in a dale '

and the old woman in the Tiecelin story lives in a valley at the foot of a mountain with a wood close by.

CICERO'S *De Divinatione*

The discourse on dreams includes two narratives which make up between them a considerable portion of the *Nonnë Prestes Tale*.

Chaucer says that he obtained them from : ' Oon of the gretteste auctours that men rede.'

This author is Cicero and the treatise from which the dreams are derived is the *De Divinatione*.

Chaucer was probably quoting from memory because he does not repeat them precisely as they occur and the second story which Chaucer refers to as in 'the nexte chapitre after this' really comes the first. Cicero declares that both tales are frequently related by the Stoics. According to his version the hero of the first was Simonides who found a body lying unburied and piously interred it; he planned to set out upon a voyage but the dead man appeared to him in a vision and advised him not to do so since, if he sailed, he would be shipwrecked; Simonides accepted the warning and returned but the rest perished.

'unum de Simonide: qui quum ignotum quemdam projectum mortuum vidisset, eumque humavisset, haberetque in animo navem conscendere, moneri visus est, ne id faceret, ab eo, quem sepultura affecerat; si navigasset, eum naufragio esse periturum; itaque Simonidem redisse; perisse ceteros, qui tum navigassent.'

Chaucer, it will be seen, has omitted one of the most salient features of the original narrative—that the dream-warning was given as a reward for the pious action of interment.

The second is almost precisely as Chaucer tells it: two Arcadians are travelling together and come to the city of Megara, one goes to an inn and the other lodges with a friend. When the latter is asleep his companion appears to him in a dream and beseeches him to come to his aid since the innkeeper is about to murder him; the man starts from his sleep in terror but comforts himself with reflecting that it is only a dream and lies down again; a second time his companion appears and entreats him that, though he would not aid him when living, he will at any rate avenge him dead; he declares that the innkeeper has placed his dead body in a waggon and thrown dung upon it and he begs his friend to be present at the city-gate in the morning before the waggon leaves. The friend obeys and enquires after the contents of the waggon when the waggoner flees in terror, the dead body is discovered and the innkeeper, since his crime is manifest, is given over to justice.

5-2

(b) THE NONNË PRESTES TALE AS A SATIRE

As has already been said the *Roman de Renart* had been employed, before Chaucer's time, for purposes of satire. The *Nonnë Prestes Tale* is, perhaps, the most exquisite example of his humour and it is so very largely because of the satire which is everywhere implicit.

It is, to begin with, a satire upon pedantry. Learning, as we have seen, had been introduced in certain branches of the *Roman de Renart*, particularly in *Renard le Contrefait*; this is composed, in part, of the traditional adventures of the fox but they are made an excuse for the introduction of a great deal of new material, the poem including many digressions on various subjects. The author, in especial, loves to display his learning by ascribing all sorts of out-of-the-way knowledge to his animals.

Chaucer employs these learned digressions purely for purposes of satire: it is one of the most attractive of his traits that he can stand outside of and even satirise his own weaknesses. He himself was, for his time, a learned man; like other mediaeval authors he was accustomed to make an elaborate display of authorities, he understood the trick of pedantic reference but he could also see its absurd and amusing side. It is often impossible to tell in a given passage whether he is in earnest or not. Thus, in the *Knight's Tale*, he asserts that he will not describe at length Emily's rites in worship of Diana but the reader who wishes to know their nature will find them in *Stace of Thebes*; the reader, as a matter of fact, cannot do anything of the kind; Chaucer may have been simply mistaken or he may have been, in a spirit of mischief, inventing a reference. It is certainly significant that the two most learned characters in the whole of his work, judging by the number of authorities they quote, are the Wife of Bath and the cock.

The *Nonnë Prestes Tale* is the first notable English satire upon pedantry ; it belongs to the same class as Pope's *Dunciad*, the *History of Martinus Scriblerus*, *Gulliver's Travels*, etc.

We have, to begin with, the satire upon astronomy and those astronomical methods of computing the date which were in favour at the time ; Chaucer himself frequently employed this method, none the less he ridicules its display of unnecessary learning ; his cock is more certain in his crowing than any clock in its hours, he knows ' by nature ' the best astronomical method of calculating the time, *i.e.* fifteen degrees on the equinoctial, and so crows at the most precise hourly intervals.

There is a similar satire in the elaborately ridiculous method of computing the date which is employed a little later in the poem :

> ' Whan that the monthe in which the world bigan
> That highte March...
> Was complet and passed were also
> Sin March began, thritty dayes and two.'

This seems to mean the third of May, but what a fantastic method of computing the date ! And the cock confirms it by calculating the height of the sun which at that day and hour is exactly forty-one degrees.

There follows the satire upon mediaeval medicine which consists in making the hen an authority on ' complexions,' ' humours ' and the like. This is doubly apposite, for the ladies of the time were expected to be skilled in the treatment of wounds and in the use of herbal medicines ; it was they who made the ' pharmacies ' described in the *Knight's Tale*.

> ' Fermacies of herbs and eek save
> They drunken, for they wolde hir limes have.'

We may note also that, in the *Squire's Tale*, the ring sent to Canace, as a gift suited for a great lady, helps her to this knowledge of herbs :

> ' And every gras that groweth upon rote
> She shal eek knowe, and whom it wol do bote,
> Al be his woundes never so depe and wyde.'

Thus, in representing Partlet as an authority upon this subject, Chaucer is mocking both the romances and the practice of mediaeval medicine. The latter certainly amused him to a very considerable degree. There is no mistaking the irony with which he tells us that the Doctour was a ' verray parfit practisour[1] ' because he was well skilled in astrology and therefore could choose exactly the right hour to make the leaden images which would cure his patient. Like Partlet he knows the cause of every malady :

> ' Were it of hoote or cold, or moiste or drye,
> And where engendred and of what humour.'

Chaucer next proceeds to satirise the mediaeval belief in divination by dreams and with all the more zest because he himself had, very frequently indeed, made use of the convention for his own purposes. Chantecler overwhelms Partlet with the number of great men who have put confidence in dreams and the well-attested instances of prophetic visions.

Partlet has no authority on her side except Dionysius Cato, the author of the *Disticha de Moribus*, to whom Chantecler refers with obvious contempt :

> ' daun Catoun
> That hath of wisdom such a great renoun.'

Dionysius Cato was among the moralists who were most popular in Chaucer's day though his wisdom was of a somewhat trite order, and it is certainly this to which Chantecler objects. The authors Chantecler quotes are the standard authorities on dreams as we can see from the fact that Chaucer refers to them elsewhere with perfect seriousness : we note especially Macrobius, Daniel (*i.e.* the dream of Nebuchadnezzar), and Joseph's interpretation of the dreams of Pharaoh.

[1] Prologue.

In the *Book of the Duchesse* Joseph, Macrobius and Pharaoh are all mentioned. Chaucer declares that his dream is so wonderful that Joseph and Macrobius themselves would find it difficult to interpret :

> ' No, not Joseph withouten drede,
> Of Egipte, he that redde[1] so
> The kinges meting Pharao[2]
> No more than coude the leste of us ;
> Ne nat scarsly Macrobëus
> He that wroot al th' avisioun
> That he mette, king Scipioun
> The noble man, the Affrican[3].'

Again, in the *Hous of Fame*, he declares that his dream is so wonderful :

> ' That I saye, ne Scipioun,
> Ne king Nabugodonosor,
> Pharo, Turnus, ne Elcanor
> Ne mette swich a dreem as this[4].'

The *Parlement of Foules* begins with a Proem that is practically a translation of Cicero's *Somnium Scipionis* but the long commentary written by Macrobius he apparently admired much less.

The mediaeval author was fond of strewing his work with Latin tags, often dragged in ' by the hair,' and Chaucer ridicules this in the Latin proverb quoted and ingeniously mistranslated by his cock.

> ' In principio
> Mulier est hominis confusio.'

Professional rhetoricians again have their absurd traits and Chaucer satirises their habit of embroidering the commonplace :

> ' God woot that worldly joye is sone ago ;
> And if a rethor koude faire endyte,
> He in a cronycle saufly mighte it write
> As for a soverayn notabilitee.'

---

[1] Interpreted.   [2] The dream of king Pharaoh.
[3] 280–90.   [4] 514–17.

We may compare this with the *Franklin's Prologue* where that good gentleman excuses himself for telling his tale in a bare and plain manner by declaring that he never studied rhetoric :

> ' I lerned never rethoryk certyn ;
> Thing that I speke, it moot be bare and pleyn.
> I sleep never on the mount of Parnaso,
> Ne lerned Marcus Tullius Cicero.'

Chaucer passes to an ironical discussion of the theory of predestination. Here again was a subject that he had taken quite seriously ; it had been made by Wyclif the leading philosophical question of the day. It was also one of the problems discussed most fully in Chaucer's favourite philosopher—Boethius.

He himself had discoursed upon it with entire gravity in *Troilus* and the *Knight's Tale*. But, undoubtedly, the doctrine of predestination, like most other things, can be made to show a comic side, as Swift, for instance, treated it in *A Tale of a Tub*, and Chaucer also reveals the comedy. The attack of the fox upon the cock was predestined by ' heigh imaginacioun ' and Chaucer refers the reader to the accepted authorities such as Augustine and Bishop Bradwardine. It is worthy of note that Wyclif proclaimed himself theologically and philo-sophically a follower of Augustine, that Bishop Brad-wardine was his predecessor at Oxford, as whose pupil and disciple he began his teaching. There is one passage in Chaucer which is plainly a summary of Wyclif's doctrine of the ' foresciti ' :

> ' Whether that goddes worthy forwiting
> Streyneth me nedely for to doon a thing,
> (Nedely clepe I simple necessitee)
> Or elles, if free choys be graunted me
> To do that same thing, or do it noght,
> Though god forwoot it, er that it was wroght.'

There follows next a touch of mockery on the peculiar natural histories of the time ; Chaucer refers to ' Phisio-

logus ' who knows all about the habits of mermaids and
can describe them with accuracy.

Next we have an amusing satire on Geoffrey de
Vinsauf. This was an author who wrote a treatise
entitled *Nova Poetria*, a manual to teach the art of
composing poetry with illustrative examples. There
must have been something supremely ridiculous to
Chaucer in the very conception of the manual, and the
absurdity was increased by the fact that Geoffrey's own
examples were particularly wooden and poor. Chaucer
must have deliberately caused his cock's misadventure
to fall upon a Friday, like the death of Richard I, so that
he could have an opportunity for lamenting the unlucky
nature of that day as Vinsauf had lamented it.

It was the fashion among mediaeval authors to make
numerous classical references whether appropriate or not,
often dragging them in quite absurdly. So Chaucer
compares the outcry made by his hens to all the most
famous laments of history : to the grief of the Trojan
women when Troy was sacked and king Priam slain, to
the frenzy of Hasdrubal's wife when the Romans burnt
Carthage, to the bitter outcries of the senators' wives
when Nero caused their husbands to be slain and burnt
the city.

Again, in mediaeval authors, a ' moral ' was considered
imperative and this also was often dragged in most
inappropriately ; numerous illustrations are to be found
in Chaucer's friend Gower, who compels every one of his
tales to serve a moral purpose whether it will or not.

This habit also Chaucer ridicules when he makes his
priest, after his piece of exquisite phantasy, calmly claim
the whole as a moral tale intended to show the ill effects
of listening to flattery :

> ' Lo, swich it is for to be recchelees,
> And necligent, and truste on flaterye ' ;

and, as he proceeds to point out, obviously with mischief,

everything that is written can be interpreted to have a moral meaning in some way or other :

> ' Al that writen is,
> To our doctryne it is y-write, y-wis.'

The *Nonně Prestes Tale* is not only a satire upon pedantry but also a burlesque of the popular romances of the day. For these Chaucer seems to have had little admiration and, as Legouis suggests, he probably did not know the best ; his acquaintance with really great writers—Virgil, Boccaccio and Dante—had shown him the weaknesses of the ordinary mediaeval model : its artificial character, the stereotyped list of perfections ascribed to the hero and heroine, the ideal and impossible nobility of their characters.

Chaucer himself had, as we have seen, used romantic motives and conventions, but they were treated in a very different style from the common one and, even so, Chaucer outgrows them ; his work shows a progressive advance in realism.

The wonderful beauty of Chantecler is plainly intended as a satire upon the perfections of the hero of romance :

> ' His byle was blak, and as the jeet it shoon ;
> Lyk asur were his legges, and his toon ;
> His nayles whytter than the lilie flour
> And lyk the burned gold was his colour.'

We may compare this with the description of Sir Thopas which also is a burlesque of the popular romance :

> ' Sir Thopas wex a doghty swayn,
> Whyt was his face as payndemayn[1],
>   His lippes rede as rose ;
> His rode[2] is lyk scarlet in grayn,
> And I yow telle in good certayn
>   He had a semely nose.'

Partlet is a parody on the romantic conception of the lady. She has all the qualities that the great lady should possess. She is ' courteous, discreet and debonaire,' she

---

[1] Fine bread.   [2] Complexion.

has, above all, the magical quality of charm, she has enthralled Chantecler and taken entirely captive his heart. Partlet also knows her value; like the mediaeval lady she insists upon courage in her husband; she must feel that she is wedded to a hero and, when Chantecler expresses his fear over his ominous dream, she breaks out into reproaches upon his cowardice. The dream really is terrifying but it was a convention that the hero of romance must be above all mortal weakness:

> 'Avoy!' quod she, 'fy on you, hertelees!
> Allas!' quod she, 'for, by that God above,
> Now han ye loste myn herte and al my love;
> I kan nat love a coward, by my feith.'

And she goes on to explain what her requirements in a husband are, giving a formidable list of virtues; the husband must be brave, wise and generous, able to keep a secret, he must not be niggardly, nor foolish, nor a boaster: above all and more than all he must be afraid of nothing:

> 'How dorste ye seyn for shame unto your love
> That any thing mighte make you aferd?
> Have ye no mannes herte and han a berd?'

Partlet in fact belongs to the class of ladies who are 'daungerous' and 'digne' and who expect too much. She is like those ladies who are contrasted unfavourably with the Duchess Blanche, who will order a lover to:

> 'Go hoodles to the drye see
> And come hoom by the Carrenare[1];
> And seye "Sir, be now right ware
> That I may of you here seyn
> Worship[2], or that ye come agen."'

We may also note that Chaucer ridicules the romances in his reference to the tale of Lancelot; he declares that his story is true:

---

[1] Gulf of Quarnaro.   [2] Honour

> ' This storie is al-so trewe, I undertake,
> As in the book of Launcelot de Lake,
> That wommen holde in ful gret reverence.'

There is a similar reference in the *Squire's Tale*; Chaucer will not attempt to speak of the ' subtle looks ' of the lovers for no one could describe them :

> ' No man but Launcelot and he is deed.'

We may observe that the *Nonnë Prestes Tale* is only one among a number of poems in which Chaucer represents birds as playing the part of human beings ; in the *Manciple's Tale* we have the crow which acts as a tale-bearer to Apollo, and is punished ; in the *Squire's Tale* there is the falcon which Canace succours and which is plainly a love-lorn lady in disguise, but the closest parallels are to be found in the *Hous of Fame* and in the *Parlement of Foules*.

In the *Hous of Fame* the eagle is as learned as Chantecler and Partlet ; he quotes Aristotle and dan Platon and gives a quasi-scientific explanation of the nature of sound taken from Boethius (*de Musica*); he also refers to Alexander Macedo, Daedalus and Icarus and other figures of classical mythology ; like Chantecler he refers to Chaucer's favourite *Somnium Scipionis :*

> That saw in dreme, at point devys,
> Helle and erthe and paradys.'

Again like Chantecler he is accomplished in astronomy though it takes a different form ; he knows all the constellations and remembers their histories, how they became what they were. The eagle, also, is exceedingly gracious and courteous to Chaucer.

It is in the *Parlement of Foules* that we find the closest parallels ; there birds are used to symbolise human beings ; the eagles typify the ' gentlefolk ' and are courteous, refined and delicate in their feelings. The satire upon romance is supplied by the ' water foul ' who cannot understand the elaborate love-troubles of the eagles.

The goose advises :

　'But she wol love him, lat him love another';
and the duck's advice is similar :

　'There been mo sterres, god wot, than a paire.'

In the *Parlement of Foules*, however, the sympathies of the author go mainly with the romantics and not with those who burlesque them.

IV

Grammar and Metre of Chaucer

PRONUNCIATION

Chaucer's pronunciation differed considerably from that of Modern English and his vowels are generally supposed to have had the continental values. They are:

ā　as in *father*.

ă　short variety of the above as in *ăha*.

ē　had two values, close and open ; close *ē* as in Fr. *é*, derived from A.S. *ē* or *ēo*, usually appears as *ee* in Mod. English.

　　　　A.S. *swēte*, Ch. *swete*, Mod. *sweet*.

　　'　A.S. *dēop*, Ch. *depe*, Mod. *deep*.

　　Open *é* as in Fr. *è*, from A.S. *ēa* or *ǣ*, usually appears in Mod. English as *ea*.

　　　　A.S. *hǣlan*, Ch. *hele*, Mod. *heal*.

　　　　A.S. *ēast*, Ch. *est*, Mod. *east*.

ĕ　as in Mod. English *bed*, *tell*, etc.

ī　as in Mod. English *ee* in *feed*. In Chaucer this sound is spelt either *i* or *y*. A.S. *wrītan*, Ch. *write*. A.S. *drīfan*, Ch. *dryve*.

ĭ　as in Fr. *fini*.

ō　has two sounds, close and open. Close *ō* like the *o* in *note* or in German *so*. It comes from A.S. *ō* and is usually represented in Mod. English by *oo*.

　　　　A.S. *bōc*, Ch. *boke*, Mod. English *book*.

　　　　A.S. *rōt*, Ch. *rote*, Mod. English *root*.

Open ō like the *au* of *Paul*. It is generally derived from A.S. *ā* and in Mod. English becomes *oa* or *o*.

A.S. *lār*, Ch. *lore*, Mod. English *lore*.

A.S. *brād*, Ch. *brode*, Mod. English *broad*.

ŏ as in *box*, *hot*. Before *nasals*, *n*, *m*, *ŏ* is sounded as *ŭ*.

A.S. *munuc*, Ch. *monk*, Mod. English *monk*.

ū as in *fool* or like Fr. *ou* in *vous*. It is often written *ou* but not pronounced as a diphthong : *flour*.

ŭ as in *full*.

Diphthongs.

ai, ay, ei, ey as in Mod. English *ay* in *day*, *way*, etc. Ch. *breyde*, *brayde*, *demeine*, etc.

au as in Mod. English *ou* or *ow* in *sound*, *now*, etc. Ch. *avaunt*, *faucon*, etc.

oi as in words of French origin like *boil*, *noise*, etc.

Grammar.

Nouns.

PLURAL. In Chaucer most nouns have conformed to the ordinary masculine declension (A.S. *as* plurals) and take their plural in *es* pronounced as a separate syllable : *naylès*, *hennès*, *owlès*, *wormès*, *wyvès*, etc.

Occasionally the plural is spelt *is* : *eeris*, *heeris*, *beryis*.

Nouns of French origin often form their plural in *s* only : *mirours*, *jogelours*, *auctours*, etc.

Chaucer has also relics of A.S. declensions, more numerous than in Mod. English.

NEUTER NOUNS (unchanged for the plural) : *sheep*, *neet*, *swyn*, *deer*, *hors*, *yeer*, etc.

WEAK NOUNS (taking an *en* plural): *toon*[1], *foon*[2], *been*[3], *oxen*, *hosen*, *eyen*[4], *asshen*[5], etc.

(Some of these have alternative strong forms.)

[1] Toes.   [2] Foes.   [3] Bees.   [4] Eyes.   [5] Ashes.

MUTATION NOUNS (showing vowel change): *goos, gees*; *fote, fete,* etc.

Some nouns such as *keen* (*cows*) show a combination of mutation and weak ending.

GENITIVE. In Chaucer the genitive of the noun is usually formed in *es* and pronounced as a separate syllable: *mannès, Goddès, wommennès, senatourès,* etc.

Foreign nouns ending in *s* have sometimes no special form for the genitive: *Venus children.*

In A.S. the class known as *r* nouns took no *s*: so in Chaucer, *fader soule, fader kyn.*

The A.S. fem. genitive ended in *e* and Chaucer has a number of instances: *Nonne Prestes, herte blood, lady grace,* etc.

The genitive plural of the A.S. weak noun ended in *ena* and there seems to be a relic of this in the form: *hevene king.*

DATIVE. Chaucer frequently employs the dative case; it ends in *e* which is pronounced as a separate syllable and occurs regularly after such prepositions as *at, by, in,* etc.: *in londè, in the dawenyngè, in his throtè, by kynde, of hewe,* etc.

ADJECTIVES.

PLURAL. A.S. adjectives varied their plurals in agreement with the nouns but the most common form was in *e* and this is the regular form for the plural in Chaucer: *redè lemès, redè beestès, blakè berès, blakè develès,* etc.

There are occasional though rare examples of a French adjective plural in *s*: *places delitables* (*Franklin's Tale*), *romances that been royales* (*Sir Thopas*).

DEFINITE FORM. The definite form of the adj. is used when the adj. is preceded by the definite article, by a demonstrative or possessive or agrees with a noun in the vocative case: *this fairè Pertelote, deerè brother, this samè nyght,* etc.

COMPARISON. Adjectives are compared by adding *er* or *re* (*derre*, *ferre*) for the comparative, and *est* for the superlative.

A certain number of adjs. compare by mutation: *old, elder, eldest ; long, lengra, lengest ; strong, strenger* or *strengra, strengest*.

There are also irregular adjectives:

god	*bet*	*best*
yvel	*wers*	*werste*
muchel	*mo* or *more*	*moste*
litel or *lite*	*lesse*	*leeste*
(*far*)	*fer*	*ferrest*
(*neigh*)	*neer*	*nexte*
(*fore*)		*firste*

ADVERBS.

Adverbs are frequently formed from adjectives by the addition of *e* or *ly* : *trewely, myrily, softè, sorè, loudè, privèly, boldèly*, etc. Adverbs are frequently formed from the genitive.

PRONOUNS.

PERSONAL PRONOUNS :

	First Pers. Sing.	*Second Pers. Sing.*
N.	I, ich, ik	thou
A.	me	thee
D.	me	thee
G.	my or myn	thy or thyn

(Note.—The second person singular is regularly employed when the person addressed is an inferior or on terms of familiarity.)

	First Pers. Plur.	*Second Pers. Plur.*
N.	we	ye
A.	us	you
D.	us	you
G.	oure	youre

Third Pers. Sing.

	Masc.	*Neut.*	*Fem.*
N.	he	hit, it	she
A.	him	hit, it	hire, hir
D.	him	him	hire, hir
G.	his	his	hire

Third Pers. Plural.

    N.   they
    A.   hem
    D.   hem
    G.   here, hir

(Note.—In A.S. all the forms of this pronoun began in *h* ; the *th* forms are really of Scandinavian origin ; Chaucer only employs the *th* form in the nominative.)

INDEFINITE PRONOUN. Chaucer retains the indef. pronoun *men* (corresponding to French *on* or German *man*) ; it can be distinguished from the plural of the noun by the fact that it always takes a singular verb : *or if men smoot it.*

DEMONSTRATIVE PRONOUNS. *That* has a plural *tho* (A.S. *þā*) *tho herbes*. *At the* is often contracted to *atte* : *atte thridde time.*

RELATIVE PRONOUNS. *That* is used for persons as well as for things and is both singular and plural. *Which* has a plural *whiche*.

(Notes.—*ilk* (A.S. *ælc*) means *the same* ; *thilke* (A.S. *þe+ǣlc*) ; *swich* (A.S. *swilc*) *such* ; *som* (A.S. *sum*)· *a* or *an* ; plural *some* ; *al* (A.S. *eall*), plur. *alle*, gen. plur. *aller* or *alder* ; *echoon* (A.S. *ǣlc+ān*), each one ; *everichoon* (A.S. *ǣfre+ǣlc+ān*), *everyone*.)

VERBS.

In Chaucer there are seven conjugations of strong verbs.

Class I.   Verbs with *ī* (Chaucer *ȳ*) infinitive :

	Infin.	Pret. Sing.	Pret. Plur.	P. P.
A.S.	*wrītan*	*wrāt*	*writon*	*writen*
Ch.	*wrȳte*	*wroot*	*writen*	*writen*
	rȳde	*rood*	*riden*	*riden*

Class II.   Verbs with *ēo* (Chaucer *ee*) or *ū* infinitive :

	Infin.	Pret. Sing.	Pret. Plur.	P. P.
A.S.	*cēosan*	*cēas*	*curon*	*coren*
Ch.	*cheese*	*chees*	*chosen*	*chosen*

6   w c

Class III. Verbs with infinitive in *ĕ* or *ĭ* followed by a double consonant :

	Infin.	Pret. Sing.	Pret. Plur.	P. P.
A.S.	*drincan*	*dranc*	*druncon*	*druncen*
A.S.	*helpan*	*healp*	*hulpon*	*holpen*
Ch.	*drinke*	*drank*	*dronken*	*dronken*
	helpe	*halp*	*holpen*	*holpen*

Class IV. Verbs with infinitive in *ĕ* or *ĭ* followed by a single consonant either a liquid or a nasal :

	Infin.	Pret. Sing.	Pret. Plur.	P. P.
A.S.	*beran*	*bær*	*bǣron*	*boren*
Ch.	*bere*	*bar*	*bēren*	*boren*
	come	*cam* or *coom*	*coomen*	*comen*

Class V. Verbs with infinitive in *ĕ* or *ĭ* followed by a single consonant not a liquid or a nasal :

	Infin.	Pret. Sing.	Pret. Plur.	P. P.
A.S.	*sittan*	*sæt*	*sǣton*	*seten*
Ch.	*sitte*	*sat, seet*	*seeten, seten*	*seten*

Class VI. Verbs with infinitive in *ă* :

	Infin.	Pret. Sing.	Pret. Plur.	P. P.
A.S.	*scacan*	*scōc*	*scōcon*	*scacen*
Ch.	*shake*	*shook*	*shooken*	*shaken*

Class VII. Verbs originally reduplicating; root vowels various, including *ă*, *ā*, *ō*, *ē*.

	Infin.	Pret. Sing.	Pret. Plur.	P. P.
A.S.	*feallan*	*fēoll*	*fēollon*	*feallen*
A.S.	*grōwan*	*grēow*	*grēowon*	*grōwen*
Ch.	*falle*	*fel, fil*		*fallen*
	growe	*grew*		*growen*

WEAK VERBS. **Class I.** Verbs which employ the stem vowel *e* in adding the pret. and p.p. endings on to the root :

	Infin.	Pret. Sing.	P. P.
A.S.	*derian*	*derede*	*dered*
Ch.	*dere*	*derede*	*dered*

Class II. Verbs which add the pret. and p.p. endings directly on to the root :

DIVISION A. Verbs which have the same vowel in infinitive and preterite:

	Infin.	Pret. Sing.	P. P.
A.S.	*hīeran*	*hīerde*	*hīered*
Ch.	*here*	*herde*	*herd*
Ch.	*feele*	*felte*	*felt*

DIVISION B. Verbs which have a mutated vowel in the infinitive but not in the preterite:

	Infin.	Pret. Sing.	P. P.
A.S.	*sēcean*	*sōhte*	*sōht*
Ch.	*seeken*	*soughte*	*sought*
	tellen	*tolde*	*told*

PRESENT INDICATIVE. The Chaucerian verb has endings for each of the three persons in the singular:

First Pers. *e*   Second Pers. *est*   Third Pers. *eth*

and a common ending for the plural in *en*:

First Pers.	*bere*	*ryde*
Second Pers.	*berest*	*rydest*
Third Pers.	*bereth*	*rydeth* or *rit*
Pl.	*beren*	*ryden*

(Notes.—Verbs which end in a dental often abbreviate the 3rd person: *stant* (*standeth*), *bit* (*biddeth*), *sit* (*sitteth*), etc. The plural *en* is sometimes abbreviated to *e*: *wende* (*wenden*), *pleye* (*pleyen*), *speke* (*speken*).

SUBJUNCTIVE. The subjunctive of the verb takes *e* in the three persons of the singular and *en* in the plural, the latter often abbreviated to *e*.

IMPERATIVE. The imperative singular of strong verbs is formed from the simple root: *tak heed*, *tel me anon*, etc.

In weak verbs the imperative singular ends in *e*: *shewe now*, *trille this pin*, etc.

The imperative plural ends in *eth*: *beth pacient*, *now herkneth*, etc.

INFINITIVE. The simple infinitive ends in *en* or *e*: *dauncen*, *drenchen*, *loken*, *lette*, *falle*, etc.

The dative infinitive ends in *en* or *e* and takes *to* or *for to* before it : *to goon on pilgrimages, for to seken, for to lighte*, etc.

PARTICIPLES. The present participle ends in *ing* or *inge* (*yng, ynge*). The past participle often has the prefix *y,* A.S. *ge* : *y-seyled, y-passed, y-ronne*, etc.

ANOMALOUS VERBS.

BE Pres. Sing. *am, art, is* ; Plur. *been, ben, arn.* Pret. Sing. *was, were, was* ; Plur. *weren, were.* Imp. *beeth.* P. P. *been, ben.*

CAN (*I know*) 2nd, 3rd Pers. Sing. *can ;* Pl. *connen.* Pt. *coude* (*knew, could*). P. P. *couth* (*known*).

DAR *I dare.* Pt. *dorste.*

MAY *I may.* Pl. *mowen.* Subj. *mowe.*

MOOT *I* or *he must, I* or *he may.* Pl. *moten.* Pt. *moste.*

SHALL *I* or *he shall.* Pl. *shullen.* Pt. *sholde.*

THAR *I* or *he needs.*

WIL *wol, wole* ; *I* or *he will.* Pl. *wolen* or *willen.* Pt. *wolde.*

WOOT *wōt* ; *I* or *he knows.* Pl. *witen* or *woot.* Pt. *wiste.*

METRE.

In his minor poems Chaucer employs a certain number of complex forms : roundels, triple roundels, etc.[1], but in the main portion of his work he employs three different metres ; the octosyllabic couplet, the seven-lined stanza, and the decasyllabic couplet.

The octosyllabic couplet was one of the favourite metres of the 14th century ; it was employed by Barbour, Gower and many other writers. Chaucer makes use of it mainly in his first period, in his translation of the *Roman de la Rose*, and in the *Book of the Duchesse*, also in one later poem, the *Hous of Fame*.

[1] See Introduction I.

Chaucer's seven-lined stanza was a metre which had been known before but which he was the first to make popular ; it is characteristic of the works composed in his so-called 'Italian period' and he was probably influenced in his choice of it by its similarity to Boccaccio's 'ottava rima.'

The characteristic metre of the *Canterbury Tales* is the decasyllabic couplet ; this was a favourite metre in French and had been known in English before Chaucer but his handling of it is so infinitely superior to that of any predecessor that, so far as English literature is concerned, he may be considered as practically the creator of the metre which has ever since remained one of the chief measures of English poetry.

The typical line contains five iambic feet but feminine rhymes are exceedingly numerous in Chaucer so that lines of eleven syllables are even commoner than those of ten ; it seems probable that an additional syllable is allowed at the caesura also and some critics think trisyllabic feet fairly common in all parts of the line. Professor Saintsbury believes that Chaucer permits the use of Alexandrines[1].

A peculiar feature of the heroic line in Chaucer (not permissible in later English) is that it may omit the first syllable and thus begin with a strong accent ; this not infrequently results in the line being in trochaic or falling metre throughout.

We may give some lines as illustrations :

(*a*)   Regular iambic :

'Was lỳk an hòund and wòlde han màad areèst.'

(*b*)   Eleven-syllabled, with feminine ending :

'But swich a joy was it to here hem syngĕ.'

(*c*)   With additional syllable at the caesura :

'What schulde he studie I and make himselven wood.'
'To Caunterbury I with ful devout corage.'

[1] *History of Prosody,* II. iv.

(*d*) With omission of first syllable and hence in trochaic metre :

> 'Twènty bòkes clàd in blàk and reèd.'
> 'Fòr to dèlen wìth no swìch poraìllè.'

(*e*) With reversal of stress in first syllable :

> 'Rìght in the nèxtë chàpitre àfter thìs.'

(*f*) An Alexandrine :

> 'Westward | right swìch | another in | the opposite.'

A great deal of the melody of Chaucer's lines depends on the proper treatment of final *e*. Elision is very frequent and takes place in the following cases :

(1) When final *e* is followed by a vowel.

(2) When final *e* is followed by a French word beginning with silent *h* or an English pronoun with an unemphatic *h* : *his, him, hit*, etc.

(3) In frequently occurring verbs such as *come, were, nolde, wolde, have*, the *e* is usually ignored. *Coude* is a difficult form because the *e* is quite irregular, so is *hadde*.

(4) *e* is usually elided in weak syllables followed by a vowel, weak syllables being *er, el, en, ed*, etc.

Examples :

(1)   'But I ne kan nat bultẹ it to the bren.'
     'Ther as he was ful myriẹ and wel at ese.'
     'Certes, it was of hertẹ, al that he song.'

(2)   'And whan that Pertẹlote thus herdẹ hym rore.'
     'Seydẹ he nat thus "Ne do no fors of dremes." '
     'And brendẹ hirselven with a stedefast herte.'

(3)   'By God, I haddë levere than my sherte
     That ye haddẹ red his legende as have I.'
     'That he haddẹ met that dreem that I yow tolde.'
     'Than wolde I shewe you how that I koudẹ pleyne.'

(4)   'Swevẹnes engendren of replecciouns.'
     'As for a sovẹrayn notabilitee.'
     'So hydous was the noys, a benẹdicịtee.'

THE NONNË PRESTES TALE

CANTERBURY TALES

THE PROLOGUE OF THE NONNË
PRESTES TALE

'Hoo!' quod the knyght, 'good sire, namoore of this
That ye han seyd is right ynough, ywis,
And muchel moore; for litel heuynesse
Is right ynough to muché folk, I gesse.
I seye for me it is a greet disese,　　　　　5
Where as men han been in greet welthe and ese,
To heeren of hire sodeyn fal, allas!
And the contrarie is ioye and greet solas,
As whan a man hath ben in poure estaat,
And clymbeth vp, and wexeth fortunat,　　　　10
And there abideth in prosperitee;
Swich thyng is gladsom, as it thynketh me,
And of swich thyng, were goodly for to telle.'
'Ye,' quod oure hoost, 'by seïnt Poulés belle!
Ye seye right sooth; this Monk he clappeth lowde;
He spak how "Fortune couered with a clowde" 16
I noot neuere what, and also of a "Tragédie"
Right now ye herde, and, pardee, no remédie
It is for to biwaillé, ne compleyne
That that is doon; and als, it is a peyne　　　　20
As ye han seyd, to heere of heuynesse.
Sire Monk, namoore of this, so god yow blesse!
Youre tale anoyeth all this compaignye;
Swich talkyng is nat worth a boterflye,
ffor ther-inne is ther no desport ne game.　　　　25

Wherfore, sire Monk, daun Piers by youre name,
I pray yow hertely, telle vs somwhat elles,
ffor sikerly nere clynkyng of youre belles,
That on youre bridel hange on euery syde,
By heuene kyng, that for vs allé dyde!   30
I sholde er this han fallen doun for sleepe,
Al-thogh the slough had neuer been so deepe;
Thanne hadde your tale al be toold in veyn,
ffor certeinly, as that thise clerkés seyn,
Where as a man may haue noon audience,   35
Noght helpeth it to tellen his sentence;
And wel I woot the substance is in me,
If any thyng shal wel reported be.
Sir, sey somwhat of huntyng, I yow preye.
'Nay!' quod this Monk, 'I haue no lust to pleye; 40
Now lat another telle, as I haue toold.'
Thanne spak oure hoost with rudé speche and boold,
And seyde vn-to the Nonnés preest anon,
'Com neer, thou preest, com hyder, thou sir Iohn.
Telle vs swich thyng as may oure hertés glade; 45
Be blithé, though thou ryde vp-on a jade.
What thogh thyn hors be bothé foule and lene?
If he wol serue thee, rekké nat a bene;
Looke that thyn herte be murie eueremo.'
'Yis, sir,' quod he, 'yis, hoost, so moot I go, 50
But I be myrie, ywis I wol be blamed.'
And right anon his tale he hath attamed,
And thus he seyde vn-to vs euerichon
This sweeté preest, this goodly man, sir Iohn.

Explicit

[8 *lines blank in the MS.*]

HEERE BIGYNNETH THE NONNES PREESTES
   TALE OF THE COK AND HEN CHAUNTE-
   CLEER AND PERTELOTE

A poure wydwé, somdel stape in age,   55
Was whilom dwellyng in a narwe cotage
Beside a greué, stondynge in a dale.
This wydwe of which I tellé yow my tale,
Syn thilké day that she was last a wyf,
In paciénce ladde a ful symple lyf,   60
ffor litel was hir catel and hir rente.
By housbondrie of swich as God hire sente
She foond hirself, and eek hire doghtren two.
Thre largé sowés hadde she, and namo;
Three keen and eek a sheep that highté Malle. 65
fful sooty was hir bour, and eek hire halle,
In which she eet ful many a sklendre meel;
Of poynaunt sauce hir neded neuer a deel.
No deyntee morsel passéd thurgh hir throte,
Hir diete was accordant to hir cote;   70
Repleccion ne made hire neuere sik,
Attempree diete was al hir phisik,
And exercise, and hertés suffisaunce.
The gouté lette hire no-thyng for to daunce,
Napoplexïe shenté nat hir heed;   75
No wyn ne drank she, neither whit ne reed;
Hir bord was seruéd moost with whit and blak,—
Milk and broun breed,—in which she foond no lak;
Seynd bacon and somtyme an ey or tweye,
ffor she was, as it were, a maner deye.   80
   A yeerd she hadde, encloséd al aboute
With stikkés, and a dryé dych with-oute,

In which she hadde a cok, heet Chauntéclcer.
In al the land of crowyng nas his peer.
His voys was murier than the murie orgon   85
On messédayes that in the chirché gon;
Wel sikerer was his crowyng in his logge
Than is a clokke, or an abbey orlogge.
By nature he knew eche ascencioun
Of the equynoxial in thilké toun;   90
ffor whan degreés fiftene weren ascended,
Thanne crew he that it myghte nat been amended.
His coomb was redder than the fyn coral,
And batailled as it were a castel wal;
His byle was blak, and as the jeet it shoon;   95
Lyk asure were hise leggés and his toon;
Hise naylés whiter than the lylye flour,
And lyk the burnéd gold was his colour.
   This gentil cok hadde in his gouernaunce
Seuene hennés for to doon al his plesaunce,   100
Whiche were hise sustrés and his paramours,
And wonder lyk to hym, as of colours;
Of whiche the faireste hewéd on hir throte
Was clepéd faire damoysele Pertélote,
Curteys she was, discreet and debonaire,   105
And compaignable, and bar hyr self so faire
Syn thilké day that she was seuen nyght oold,
That trewély she hath the herte in hoold
Of Chauntécleer, loken in euery lith;
He loued hire so that wel was hym therwith;   110
But swiche a ioye was it to here hem synge,
Whan that the brighté sonne bigan to sprynge,
In sweete accord, 'My lief is faren in londe';
ffor thilké tyme as I haue vnderstonde,

Beestés and briddés koudé speke and synge.   115
And so bifel that in a¹ dawénynge
As Chauntécleer among hise wyués alle
Sat on his perché, that was in the halle,
And next hym sat this fairé Pertelote,
This Chauntécleer gan gronen in his throte,   120
As man that in his dreem is drecchéd soore.
And whan that Pertelote thus herde hym roore,
She was agast, and seyde, 'O herté deere!
What eyleth yow, to grone in this manére?
Ye been a verray sleper; fy, for shame!'   125
     And he answerde and seydé thus 'Madame,
I pray yow that ye take it nat agrief;
By God me mette² I was in swich meschief
Right now, that yet myn herte is soore afright.
Now God,' quod he, ' my sweuene recche aright,   130
And kepe my body out of foul prisoun!
Me mette how that I roméd vp and doun
With-inne our yeerd wheer as I saugh a beest
Was lyk an hound, and wolde han maad areest
Vpon my body, and han had me deed.   135
His colour was bitwixé yelow and reed,
And tippéd was his tayl and bothe hise eeris,
With blak, vnlyk the remenant of hise heeris;
His snowté smal, with glowynge eyen tweye.
Yet of his look, for feere almoost I deye;   140
This causéd me my gronyng doutélees.'
     'Avoy!' quod she, ' fy on yow, hertélees!
Allas!' quod she, 'for by that God aboue!
Now han ye lost myn herte and al my loue
I kan nat loue a coward, by my feith!   145
                    ¹ H.   ² H etc.

ffor certés, what so any womman seith,
We alle desiren, if it myghté bee,
To han housbóndes hardy, wise, and free,
And secree, and no nygard, ne no fool,
Ne hym that is agast of euery tool,   150
Ne noon auauntour, by that god aboue!
How dorste ye seyn, for shame, vn-to youre loue
That any thyng myghte maké yow aferd?
Haue ye no mannés herte and han a berd?
    'Allas! and konne ye been agast of sweuenys? 155
No thyng, God woot, but vanitee in sweuene is.
Sweuenes engendren of repleccions,
And ofte of fume, and of compleccions,
Whan humours been to habundant in a wight.
Certés this dreem, which ye han met to-nyght, 160
Cometh of the[1] greet superfluytee
Of youré redé colera, pardee,
Which causeth folk to dreden in hir dremes
Of arwés, and of fyre with redé lemes,
Of greté beestés, that they wol hem byte,   165
Of contekes and of whelpés, grete and lyte;
Right as the humour of malencolie
Causeth ful many a man in sleepe to crie,
ffor feere of blaké beres or bolés blake,
Or ellés blaké deueles wole hem take.   170
Of othere humours koude I telle also
That werken many a man in sleepe ful wo;
But I wol passe as lightly as I kan.
Lo, Caton, which that was so wys a man,
Seyde he nat thus, " ne do no fors of dremes?" 175
    'Now, sire,' quod she, 'whan ye flee fro thise[2] bemes,

¹ H.   ² H.

ffor Goddés loue, as taak som laxatyf.
Vp peril of my soule, and of my lyf,
I conseille yow the beste, I wol nat lye,
That bothe of colere and of malencolye   180
Ye purgé yow, and for ye shal nat tarie,
Though in this toun is noon apothecarie,
I shal my self to herbés techen yow
That shul been for youre hele, and for youre prow ;
And in oure yeerd tho herbés shal I fynde   185
The whiche han of hire propretee by kynde
To purgé yow, bynethe and eek aboue.
fforyet nat this, for Goddés owcné loue I
Ye been ful coleryk of compleccion.
Waré the sonne in his ascencion   190
Ne fynde yow nat repleet of humours hoote;
And if it do I dar wel leye a grote
That ye shul haue a ffeuere terciane,
Or an agu, that may be youre bane.
A day or two ye shul haue digestyues   195
Of wormés, er ye take youre laxatyues
Of lawriol, centaure and ffumetere,
Or elles of ellébor that groweth there,
Of katapuce or of gaitrys beryis   199
Of herbe yue, growyng in oure yeerd, ther mery is ;
Pekke hem vp right as they growe and ete hem yn ;
Be myrie, housbonde, for youre fader kyn !
Dredeth no dreem ; I kan sey yow namoore.'
    'Madame,' quod he, '*graunt mercy* of youre loore,
But nathélees, as touchyng Daun Catoun.   205
That hath of wysdom swich a greet renoun,
Though that he bad no dremes for to drede,
By God, men may in oldé bookés rede

Of many a man, moore of auctorite,
Than euere Caton was, so moot I thee!   210
That al the reuers seyn of this sentence,
And han wel founden by experience
That dremés been significacions
As wel of joye as of tribulacions
That folk enduren in this lif present.   215
Ther nedeth make of this noon argument,
The verray preeué sheweth it in dede.

Oon of the gretteste auctours[1] that men rede
Seith thus, that whilom two felawés wente
On pilgrimage, in a ful good entente,   220
And happéd so they coomen in a toun,
Wher as ther was swich congregacioun
Of peple, and eek so streit of herbergage,
That they ne founde as muche as o cotage
In which they bothé myghté loggéd bee;   225
Wherfore they mosten of necessitee,
As for that nyght, departen compaignye;
And ech of hem gooth to his hostelrye,
And took his loggyng as it woldé falle.
That oon of hem was loggéd in a stalle,   230
ffer in a yeerd, with oxen of the plough;
That oother man was loggéd wel ynough,
As was his auenture or his ffortune,
That vs gouerneth alle as in commune.

And so bifel that longe er it were day,   235
This man mette in his bed, ther as he lay,
How that his felawe gan vp-on hym calle,
And seyde, "Allas! for in an oxes stalle
This nyght I shal be mordred ther I lye;
[1] Cam.

Now helpe me, deeré brother, or I dye;   240
In allé hasté com to me!" he sayde.
  This man out of his sleepe for feere abrayde;
But whan that he was wakened of his sleepe,
He turnéd hym and took of this[1] no keepe;
Hym thoughte his dreem nas but a vanitee.   245
Thus twiés in his slepyng dremed hee,
And atté thriddé tyme yet his felawe
Cam, as hym thoughte, and seide, "I am now slawe!
Bihoold my bloody woundés, depe and wyde;
Arys vp erly in the morwé tyde,   250
And at the west gate of the toun," quod he,
"A carte ful of donge ther shaltow se,
In which my body is hid ful priuély;
Do thilké carte arresten boldély;
My gold causéd my mordré, sooth to sayn."   255
And tolde hym euery point how he was slayn,
With a ful pitous facé, pale of hewe;
And trusté wel, his dreem he foond ful trewe;
ffor on the morwe, as soone as it was day,
To his felawés in he took the way,   260
And whan that he cam to this oxes stalle,
After his felawe he bigan to calle.
  The hostiler answerdé hym anon
And seydé, "Sire, your felawe is agon;
As soone as day he wente out of the toun.'   265
  This man gan fallen in suspecioun,—
Remembrynge on hise dremés, that he mette,—
And forth he gooth, ne lenger wolde he lette,
Vn-to the westgate of the toun, and fond
A dong carte, as it were to dongé lond,   270

          [1] H etc.

That was arrayéd in that samé wise
As ye han herd the dedé man deuyse;
And with an hardy herte he gan to crye
Vengeance and justice of this felonye.
"My felawe mordred is this samé nyght,   275
And in this carte[1] he lith gapyng upright
"I crye out on the ministres," quod he,
"That sholden kepe and reulen this citee;
Harrow! allas! heere lith my felawe slayn!"

    What sholde I moore vn-to this talé sayn?   280
The peple out sterte and caste the cart to grounde,
And in the myddel of the dong they founde
The dedé man, that mordred was al newe.
O blisful God, that art so just and trewe!
Lo, howe that thou biwreyest mordre alway!   285
Mordré wol out, that se we day by day;
Mordre is so wlatsom, and abhomynable
To God, that is so just and resonable,
That he ne wol nat suffre it heléd be,
Though it abyde a yeer, or two, or thre;   290
Mordré wol out, this my conclusioun.
And right anon. ministres of that toun
Han hent the carter, and so soore hym pyned,
And eek the hostiler so soore engyned,
That they biknewe hire wikkednesse anon,   295
And were an-hanged by the nekké bon.

    Heere may men seen that dremes been to drede;
And certés, in the samé book I rede,
Right in the nexté chapitre after this,—
I gabbé nat, so haue I ioye or blis,—   300
Two men that wolde han passéd ouer see,

---

[1] E and H insert ' heere.'   Four MSS. omit.

ffor certeyn cause in to a fer contrée
If that the wynd ne haddé been contrarie,
That made hem in a citee for to tarie
That stood ful myrie vpon an hauen syde;   305
But on a day, agayn the euen-tyde,
The wynd gan chaunge, and blew right as hem leste.
Iolif and glad they wente vn-to hir reste,
And casten hem ful erly for to saille.
But[1] to that o man fil a greet meruaille;
That oon of hem in slepyng as he lay,   311
Hym mette a wonder dreem, agayn the day;
Him thoughte a man stood by his beddés syde
And hym comanded that he sholde abyde,
And seyde hym thus: " If thou tomorwé wende, 315
Thow shalt be dreynt, my tale is at an ende."

He wook, and tolde his felawe what he mette,
And preydé hym his viage to lette;
As for that day, he preydé hym to byde.
His felawe, that lay by his beddés syde,   320
Gan for to laughe, and scornéd him ful faste;
"No dreem," quod he, "may so myn herte agaste,
That I wol letté for to do my thynges;
I setté nat a straw by thy dremynges,
ffor sweuenes been but vanytees and japes;   325
Men dreme al day of owlés or of apes,
And of many a mazé ther-with-al;
Men dreme of thyng that neuere was ne shal;
But sith I see that thou wolt heere abyde,
And thus forslewthen wilfully thy tyde,   330
God woot it reweth me, and haue good day!"
And thus he took his leue, and wente his way;

[1] E inserts ' herkneth.'

But er that he hadde half his cours yseyled,
Noot I nat why, ne what myschaunce it eyled,
But casuelly the shippés botmé rente,   335
And shipe and man vnder the water wente
In sighte of othere shippés it bisyde,
That with hem seyléd at the samé tyde!
And therfore, fairé Pertélote so deere,
By swiche ensamplés oldé[1] maistow leere,   340
That no man sholdé been to recchelees
Of dremés, for I seye thee doutélees,
That many a dreem ful soore is for to drede.
  Lo! in the lyf of Seint Kenelm I rede,
That was Kenulphus sone, the noble kyng   345
Of Mercenrike[2], how Kenelm mette a thyng
A lite er he was mordred, on a day
His mordre in his auysion he say.
His norice hym expownéd euery deel
His sweuene, and bad hym for to kepe hym weel
ffor traison; but he nas but .vij. yeer oold,   351
And therfore litel talé hath he toold
Of any dreem, so hooly is his herte.
By God, I haddé leuere than my sherte
That ye hadde rad his legende as haue I.   355
Dame Pertélote, I sey yow trewély,
Macrobeus, that writ the avision
In Affrike of the worthy Cipion
Affermeth dremés and seïth that they been
Warnynge of thyngés that men after seen;   360
And forther-moore, I pray yow looketh wel
In the Olde Testament of Daniel,
If he heeld dremés any vanitee.

---

[1] E inserts 'yet' H and others omit.   [2] Lans

Reed eek of Ioseph, and ther shul ye see
Wher dremés be somtyme,—I sey nat alle—   365
Warnynge of thyngés that shul after falle.
Looke of Egipte the kyng, daun Pharao,
His baker and his butiller also,
Wher they ne felté noon effect in dremes.
Who so wol seken actes of sondry remes   370
May rede of dremés many a wonder thyng.
  Lo, Cresus, which that was of Lydé kyng
Mette he nat that he sat vp-on a tree,
Which signified he sholde anhanged bee?
  Lo heere Adromacha, Ectorés wyf,   375
That day that Ector sholdé lese his lyf,
She dreméd on the samé nyght biforn
How that the lyf of Ector sholde be lorne,
If thilké day he wente in-to bataille;
She warnéd hym, but it myghte nat auaille;   380
He wenté for to fighté nathéles,
But he was slayn anon of Achilles;
But thilké tale is al to longe to telle,
And eek it is ny day, I may nat dwelle;
Shortly I seye, as for conclusion,   385
That I shal han of this Avision
Aduersitee; and I seye forthermoor
That I ne telle of laxatyues no stoor,
ffor they been venymés, I woot it weel;
I hem diffye, I loue hem neuer a deel!   390
  Now let vs speke of myrthe, and stynte al this;
Madamé Pertélote, so haue I blis,
Of o thyng God hath sent me largé grace;
ffor whan I se the beautee of youre face
Ye been so scarlet reed aboute youre eyen,   395
It maketh al my dredé for to dyen,

ffor al so siker as "*In principio*
Mulier est hominis confusio"
Madame, the sentence of this Latyn is,
"Womman is mannés joye and al his blis";   400
ffor whan I feele a nyght your softe syde

. . . .

I am so ful of ioye and of solas,
That I diffyé bothé sweuene and dreem";   405
And with that word he fly doun fro the beem,
ffor it was day, and eke hise hennés alle ;
And with a chuk he gan hem for to calle,
ffor he hadde founde a corn, lay in the yerd.
Réal he was, he was namoore aferd,   410

. .. .

He looketh as it were a grym leoun,
And on hise toos he rometh vp and doun ;
Hym deignéd nat to sette his foot to grounde. 415
He chukketh whan he hath a corn yfounde,
And to hym rennen thanne hise wyués alle ;
Thus roial as a prince is in his[1] halle,
Leue I this Chauntécleer in his pasture,
And after wol I telle his áuenture.   420
Whan that the monthe in which the world bigan,
That highté March, whan God first makéd man,
Was compleet and passéd were also
Syn March bigan, thritty dayés and two
Bifel that Chauntécleer in al his pryde,   425
Hise seuene wyués walkynge by his syde,
Caste vp hise eyen to the brighté sonne
That in the signe of Taurus haddé yronne
Twenty degrees and oon, and som-what moore
And knew by kynde, and by noon oother loore,   430

[1] H.

That it was pryme and crew with blisful steuene
'The sonne,' he seyde, 'is clomben vp on heuene
ffourty degrees and oon, and moore ywis.
Madamé Pertélote, my worldés blis,
Herkneth thise blisful briddés how they synge,   435
And se the fresshé flourés how they sprynge
fful is myn herte of reuel and solas!'
But sodeynly hym fil a sorweful cas;
ffor euere the latter ende of ioye is wo.
God woot that worldly ioye is soone ago,   440
And if a rethor koudé faire endite,
He in a cronycle saufly myghte it write,
As for a souereyn notabilitee.
Now euery wys man, lat him herkné me;
This storie is al so trewe, I vndertake,   445
As is the book of Launcelot de Lake
That wommen holde in ful greet reuerence.
Now wol I turne¹ agayn to my sentence.
   A colfox ful of sly iniquitee,
That in the groue hadde wonnéd yerés three,   450
By heigh ymaginacion forn-cast,
The samé nyght thurgh-out the heggés brast
In-to the yerd, ther Chauntécleer the faire
Was wont, and eek hise wyués, to repaire;
And in a bed of wortés stille he lay,   455
Til it was passéd vndren of the day,
Waitynge his tyme on Chauntécleer to falle;
As gladly doon thise homycidés alle
That in await liggen to mordré men.
   O falsé mordrour lurkynge in thy den!   460
O newé Scariot, newé Genylon!

¹ H etc.

ffalsé dissimilour[1] o Greek Synon
That broghtest Troye al outrély to sorwe !
O Chauntécleer, acurséd be that morwe,
That thou in-to that yerd flaugh fro the bemes !   465
Thou were ful wel ywarnéd by thy dremés
That thilké day was perilous to thee ;
But what that God forwoot moot nedés bee,
After the opinion of certein clerkis.
Witnesse on hym that any parfit clerk is,   470
That in scole is greet altercacion
In this mateere, and greet disputison,
And hath been of an hundred thousand men ;
But I ne kan nat bulte it to the bren,
As kan the hooly doctour Augustyn,   475
Or Boece, or the Bisshope Bradwardyn,
Wheither that Goddés worthy forwityng
Streyneth me nedely for[2] to doon a thyng
Nedély clepe I symple necessitee,—
Or ellés if free choys be graunted me   480
To do that samé thyng, or do it noght,
Though God forwoot it er that it was wroght ;
Or if his wityng streyneth neuer a deel,
But by necessitee condicioneel.
I wil nat han to do of swich mateere,   485
My tale is of a cok, as ye may heere,
That took his conseil of his wyf with sorwe,
To walken in the yerd vpon that morwe
That he hadde met that dreem that I yow[3] tolde
Wommennés conseils been ful ofté colde ;   490
Wommannés conseil broghte vs first to wo
And made Adam fro[4] Paradys to go,

---

[1] H etc.   [2] H etc.   [3] H etc.   [4] H etc.

Ther as he was ful myrie and wel at ese;
But for I noot to whom it myght displese,
If I conseil of wommen woldé blame   495
Passe ouer, for I seye it in my game.
Rede auctours where they trete of swich mateere,
And what they seyn of wommen ye may heere;
Thise been the cokkés wordés, and nat myne,
I kan noon harm of no womman diuyne.   500
   Faire in the soond, to bathe hire myrily,
Lith Pertélote, and alle hire sustres by,
Agayn the sonne, and Chauntécleer so free
Soong murier than the mermayde in the see;
ffor Phisiologus seith sikerly,   505
How that they syngen wel and myrily.
   And so bifel that as he cast his eye
Among the wortés, on a boterflye,
He was war of this fox that lay ful lowe.
No-thyng ne liste hym thanné for to crowe,   510
But cride anon, 'Cok cok!' and vp he sterte,
As man that was affrayéd in his herte,—
ffor natureelly, a beest desireth flee
ffro his contrarie, if he may it see,
Though he neuer erst hadde seyn it with his eye.
   This Chauntecleer, whan he gan hym espye,   516
He wolde han fled, but that the fox anon
Seyde, 'Gentil sire, allas! wher wol ye gon?
Be ye affrayed of me that am youre freend?
Now certés, I were worsé than a feend,   520
If I to yow wolde harm or vileynye.
I am nat come your conseil for tespye,
But trewély the cause of my comynge
Was oonly for to herkne how that ye synge;

ffor trewély, ye haue as myrie a steuene   525
As any aungel hath[1] that is in heuene
Ther-with ye han in musyk moore feelynge
Than hadde Boece, or any that kan synge.
My lord youre fader,—God his soulé blesse!
And eek youre mooder, of hire gentillesse,   530
Han in myn hous ybeen to my greet ese,
And certés, sire, ful fayn wolde I yow plese.
But for men speke of syngyng, I wol[2] seye—
So moote I brouké wel myne eyen tweye,—
Saue yow, herde I neuere man yet synge   535
As dide youre fader in the morwenynge.
Certés, it was of herte, al that he song;
And for to make his voys the mooré strong,
He wolde so peyne hym that with bothe hise eyen
He mosté wynke, so loude he woldé cryen;   540
And stonden on his tiptoon ther-with-al,
And strecché forth his nekké, long and smal;
And eek he was of swich discrecion
That ther nas no man in no region
That hym in song or wisedom myghté passe.   545
I haue wel rad, in " Daun Burnel the Asse"
Among hise vers, how that ther was a cok,
ffor that a preestés sone yaf hym a knok
Vp-on his leg, whil he was yong and nyce,
He made hym for to lese his benefice;   550
But certeyn ther nys no comparison
Bitwixe the wisedom and discrecion
Of youré fader and of his subtiltee.
Now syngeth, sire, for seinté charitee;
Lat se, konne ye youre fader countrefete.'   555

          [1] H etc.   [2] E inserts ' yow.'

This Chauntécleer hise wyngés gan to bete,
As man that koude his trayson nat espie,
So was he rauysshed with his flaterie.
  Allas, ye lordés, many a fals flatour
Is in youre courtes, and many a losengeour,   560
That plesen yow wel mooré, by my feith,
Than he that soothfastnesse vn-to yow seith,—
Redeth Ecclesiaste of flaterye,—
Beth war, ye lordés, of hir trecherye.
  This Chauntécleer stood hye vp on his toos   565
Strecchynge his nekke, and heeld hise eyen cloos,
And gan to crowé loudé for the nones,
And daun Russell, the fox, stirte vp atones,
And by the gargat henté Chauntécleer,
And on his bak toward the wode hym beer ;   570
ffor yet ne was ther no man that hym sewed.
O destinee that mayst nat been eschewed !
Allas that Chauntécleer fleigh fro the bemes !
Allas, his wyf ne roghté nat of dremes !
And on a Friday fil al this meschaunce.   575
  O Venus, that art goddesse of plesaunce,
Syn that thy seruant was this Chauntécleer
And in thy seruyce dide al his poweer,
Moore for delit than world to multiplye,
Why woltestow suffre hym on thy day to dye ?   580
O Gaufred, deeré maister souerayn,
That, whan thy worthy kyng Richard was slayn
With shot, compleynedest his deeth so soore !
Why ne hadde I now thy sentence, and thy loore,
The Friday for to chide, as diden ye ?—   585
ffor on a Friday, soothly, slayn was he.
Thanne wolde I shewe yow how that I koude pleyne

ffor Chauntécleers drede, and for his peyne,
    Certés, swich cry, ne lamentacion
Was neuere of ladyes maad whan Ylion   590
Was wonne, and Pirrus with his streité swerd,
Whan he hadde hent kyng Priam by the berd,
And slayn hym—as seith vs *Eneydos*—
As maden alle the hennés in the clos,
Whan they had seyn of Chauntécleer the sighte.   595
But sovereynly[1] dame Pertéloté shrighte,
fful louder than dide Hasdrubalés wyf,
Whan that hir housbonde haddé lost his lyf,
And that the Romayns haddé brend Cartage,—
She was so ful of torment and of rage,   600
That wilfully in-to the fyr she sterte,
And brende hir seluen with a stedefast herte.
O woful hennés, right so criden ye,
As, whan that Nero brendé the citee
Of Romé, cryden the[2] senatours wyues   605
ffor that hir husbondes losten alle hir lyues
With-outen gilt,—this Nero hath hem slayn.
Now wol I torné[3] to my tale agayn.
    This sely wydwe, and eek hir doghtrés two,
Herden thise hennés crie and maken wo,   610
And out at dorés stirten they anon
And syen the fox toward the groué gon,
And bar vp-on his bak the cok away,
And cryden, "Out! harrow! and weylaway!
Ha! ha! the fox!" and after hym they ran,   615
And eek with staués many another man;
Ran Colle oure dogge, and Talbot and Gerland
And Malkyn, with a dystaf in hir hand;

            [1] H.   [2] H etc.   [3] H etc.

Ran cow and calf and eek[1] the verray hogges,
Soré aferd[2] for berkyng of the dogges   620
And shoutyng of the men and wommen eek;
They ronné so hem thoughte hir herte breek.
They yolléden, as feendés doon in helle;
The dokés cryden, as men wolde hem quelle;
The gees, for feeré, flowen ouer the trees;   625
Out of the hyvé cam the swarm of bees;
So hydous was the noyse, *a benedicitee*!
Certés, he Iakke Straw, and his meynee,
Ne made neuere shoutés half so shrille,
Whan that they wolden any Flemyng kille,   630
As thilké day was maad vp-on the fox.
Of bras they broghten bemés, and of box,
Of horn, of boon, in whiche they blewe and powped,
And ther-with-al they skrikéd and they howped;
It seméd as that heuene sholdé falle.   635
    Now, goodé men, I pray yow herkneth alle;
Lo, how Fortune turneth sodeynly
The hope and pryde eek[3] of hir enemy!
This cok, that lay vpon the foxes bak,
In al his drede vn-to the fox he spak,   640
And seyde, 'Sire if that I were as ye,
Yet wolde I seyn, as wys god helpé me,
"Turneth agayn, ye proudé cherlés alle!
A verray pestilence vp-on yow falle;
Now am I come vn-to the wodés syde,   645
Maugree youre heed, the cock shal heere abyde;
I wol hym ete in feith, and that anon."'
    The fox answerde, 'In feith it shal be don';
And as he spak that word, al sodeynly
This Cok brak from his mouth delyuerly,   650

[1] H etc.   [2] Lans. etc.   [3] H.

And heighe vp-on a tree he fleigh anon,
And whan the fox saugh that he was ygon,--
'Allas!' quod he, O Chauntécleer! allas!
I haue to yow,' quod he, 'ydoon trespas,
In as muche as I makéd yow aferd   655
Whan I yow hente and broght out of the¹ yerd;
But, sire, I dide it of no wikke entente.
Com doun, and I shal telle yow what I mente;
I shal seye sooth to yow, God help me so!'
    'Nay thanne,' quod he, 'I shrewe vs bothé two, 660
And first I shrewe my self, bothe blood and bones,
If thou bigyle me any ofter than ones
Thou shalt na mooré, thurgh thy flaterye,
Do me to synge, and wynké with myn eye,
ffor he that wynketh, whan he sholdé see,   665
Al wilfully, God lat him neuere thee!'
'Nay,' quod the fox, 'but God yeue hym meschaunce,
That is so vndiscreet of gouernaunce
That jangleth whan he sholdé holde his pees.
Lo, swich it is for to be recchélees,   670
And necligent, and truste on flaterye.
But ye that holden this tale a folye,--
As of a fox or of a cok and hen,--
Taketh the moralité, goode men;
ffor Seint Paul seith that al that writen is,   675
To oure doctrine it is ywrite ywis;
Taketh the fruyt and lat the chaf be stille,
Now, goodé God, if that it be thy wille,
As seith my lord, so make vs alle goode men
And brynge vs to his heighé blisse! *Amen.*   680

    Heere is ended the Nonnes preestes tale.

¹ Lans.

NOTES

NONNË PRESTES PROLOGUE

1. good sire : the Monk has just been narrating his tale which
consists of a series of tragedies, beginning with Lucifer and Adam
and coming down to his own contemporaries. The kind-hearted
Knight cannot bear its melancholy and hence interrupts.

It is worthy of note that the *Nonnë Prestes Tale* makes several
references to the *Monk's Tale*: Nabugodonosor (*Nonnë Prestes
Tale*, 308), Nero (*N.P.T.* 550–2), Cresus (*N.P.T.* 318–20).

17. Tragedie : the Host quotes the fine-sounding word with
some irony. The *Monk's Tale* is probably early work, and in
these strictures Chaucer seems to be quoting his own final
criticism.

21. to heere of heuynesse : to listen to tragedy.

25. no desport ne game : no pleasure or jest.

27. hertely : sincerely.

28. clynkyng of youre belles. Cf. *Prologue*, Monk :

'And when he rood, men mighte his brydel here
Ginglen in a whistling wind as clere
And eek as loude as dooth the chapel-belle
Ther, as this lord was keper of a celle.'

32. the slough : the roads in the 14th century were extremely
bad and ill-kept.

36. his sentence : his tale or story.

37. the substance is in me : the Host means that he certainly
has the power to listen if a tale is a sufficiently good narrative.

39. **somwhat of huntyng**: the Monk's favourite pursuit was hunting. Cf. *Prologue* :

'He yaf nat of that text a pulled hen
That seith, that hunters been nat holy men ;

Greyhoundes he hadde, as swifte as fowel in flight,
Of priking and of hunting for the hare
Was al his lust, for no cost wolde he spare.'

The Monk is, however, annoyed by this allusion to his neglect of religion and will say no more. See also Introduction I.

40. **I haue no lust to pleye** : I am not in the mood for jesting.

44. **sir Iohn** : a common form of address for a priest.

46. **a jade** : a poor horse.

48. **rekké nat a bene** : care nothing.

51. **But I be myrie** : unless I am merry.

52. **attamed** : broached, started.

55. **stape in age** : advanced in years.

56. **whilom**: formerly or once upon a time : A.S. hwīlum (from time to time).

58. **yow** : A.S. ēow, dative.

59. **thilke** : A.S. þē and ælc : a demonstrative equivalent to 'that.'

61. **catel** : property, possessions. M.E. chattels.
rente : income.

62. **housbondrie** : economy.

63. **foond hirself** : found, i.e. provided for herself.

doghtrēn : this is an 'r' noun in A.S. : and forms its plural by mutation : M.E. adds the 'n' of the weak plural.

65. **keen**: cows. A.S. cū : cȳ. M.E. here also adds the 'n' of the weak ending.

66. **fful sooty was hir bour, and eek hire halle** : the outer room was called the 'hall' and the inner the 'bour' ; Chaucer was probably using the terms ironically as they suggest a much larger house than the one he had in mind. They were both 'sooty' because the house had no chimney ; it would be a rough two-roomed cottage, the poultry occupying the outer room and the widow and her two daughters the inner one.

68. **poynaunt sauce.** Sauce seems to have played a large part

in the dietary of Chaucer's day; it is always alluded to as associated with good eating. We may compare the Franklin (*Prologue*):

> ' Wo was his cook, but if his sauce were
>   Poynaunt and sharp.'

70. accordant to hir cote: according to her cottage.

72. Attempree diete: moderate diet.

73. hertes suffisaunce: contentment of heart; *i.e.* she did not make herself ill with peevishness or fretting.

74. The goute lette her etc.: the gout did not hinder her from dancing: gout was supposed to be a disease caused by good living and excess.

75. Napoplexie shente nat hir heed: apoplexy did not injure (lit. 'spoil') her head.

77. with whit and blak: chosen with ironical parallel to the ' white and red ' of the preceding line.

78. broun breed: probably rye-bread.

79. Seynd bacon: singed, *i.e.* broiled bacon.

ey or tweye: the widow is so poor that even an egg is a luxury to her; this is the more striking as poultry were common enough in Chaucer's time; his favourite phrase for anything of little value was ' nat worth a hen.'

80. a maner deye: a kind of dairywoman. Perhaps suggested by the old woman in the Tiecelin story. See Introduction III.

81. yeerd: A.S. geard: an enclosed space, not paved.

82. With stikkes: another sign of extreme poverty: the fox breaks in through the weak fencing.

84. nas his peer: was not his peer or equal.

85. orgon: a plural form taking the plural verb.

87. logge: his lodge or dwelling.

88. orlogge: the great clock of an abbey.

89–90. eche ascencioun of the equynoxial: the space measured in an hour, *i.e.* fifteen degrees.

94. batailled: embattled.

96. toon: toes, a weak plural.

98. burned gold: burnished gold.

101. paramours: wives or lovers; the word has no bad sense in Chaucer or Spenser.

105. debonaire: gracious, courteous and of good manners.

106. **compaignable** : companionable, agreeable.

107. **seuen nyght** : A.S. niht, unchanged in plural.

108. **the herte in hoold**, etc. : she has taken complete possession of the heart of Chauntecleer.

in hoold : in prison.

109. **loken in euery lith** : locked in every limb. A.S. liþ : a limb or joint. A.S. liþan : to go.

112. **bigan to sprynge** : began to rise.

113. **My lief is faren in londe** : apparently the refrain of a popular song, 'my love has gone away.'

115. **briddes** : older form of bird.

116. **dawenynge** : dawning. A.S. dagian, to dawn.

118. **the halle** : the outer room.

121. **drecchéd soore** : troubled sorely. A.S. dreccan, to trouble or afflict.

124. **What eyleth yow** : an impersonal verb taking the dative.

125. **a verray sleper** : a fine sleeper (ironically).

128. **me mette** : I dreamt ; an impersonal verb which takes the dative.

in swich meschief : in such misfortune : the word had a much stronger sense in older English than it possesses now. Cf. Milton's *Comus* :

> 'Yea, even that which Mischief meant most harm
> Shall in the happy trial prove most glory.'

130. **my sweuene recche aright** : interpret my dream aright. A.S. reccan, to explain or interpret ; racu, narrative or exposition.

134. **wolde han maad areest** : wished to have seized or laid hold of.

137–8. **tipped was his tayl**, etc. : this is exactly the description of a ' colfox.'

139. **eyen** : A.S. ēagan, weak plural.

142. **Avoy** : Fy.

hertelees : without heart, *i.e.* coward.

148. **hardy** : brave, courageous.

free : generous.

149. **secree** : able to keep a secret, reliable.

150. **agast of euery tool** : afraid of every weapon.

151. **auauntour** : boaster.

155. **sweuenys** : dreams.

157. **Sweuenes engendren of repleccions** : dreams arise from excesses.

158. **And ofte of fume, etc.** : we may compare the *Squire's Tale*:

'Hir dremes shul not been y-told for me,
Ful were hir hedes of fumositee,
That causeth dreem of which ther nis no charge,'

i.e. the dreams caused by 'fumositee' are, as Partlet says, of 'no charge,' that is they have no weight or meaning. 'of complecciouns': from the natural temperament. According to mediaeval medicine there were supposed to be four 'complexions' or temperaments, *i.e.* the sanguine, choleric, melancholy, and phlegmatic. These 'complexions' of body also carried with them corresponding mental dispositions and habits of mind; hence the sense which the words still bear.

159. **humours.** Burton (*Anatomy of Melancholy*) says concerning humours :

' A humour is a liquid or fluent part of the body, comprehended in it for the preservation of it, and is either innate and born with us or adventitious and acquisite.' He goes on to explain that there are four natural humours: ' pituita or phlegm, choler and melancholy. These four humours have some analogy with the four elements.'

162. **rede colera.** Burton defines 'choler' as follows: ' Choler is hot and dry, bitter, begotten of the hotter parts of the chylus. and gathered to the gall : it helps the natural heat and senses and serves to the expelling of excrements.'

164. **lemes**: rays. A.S. leoma, ray of light, radiance.

166. **contekes**: conflicts.

167. **humour of malencolie.** Burton quotes ' Hercules de Saxonia holds these that are naturally melancholy to be of a leaden colour or black...and such as think themselves dead many times or that they see, talk with black men, dead men, spirits and goblins frequently if it be in excess.'

Cf. *Knight's Tale.* Arcite seems to suffer:

'Not only lyk the loveres maladye
Of Hereos but rather like manye
Engendred of humour malencolyk
Biforen in his celle fantastyk.'

174. **Lo, Catọn, which that was so wys a man**: Dionysius
Cato who was an author much esteemed in the Middle Ages;
he compiled a volume of moral aphorisms intended for the educa-
tion of the young and dedicated to his own son 'Ad Filium.' The
volume is entitled *Disticha de Moribus.* It begins with brief
aphorisms such as 'Convivare raro,' 'Nihil temere credideris,'
'Nihil mentire,' and proceeds to slightly longer ones—aphorisms
of two lines each. The work was well known to Chaucer and
is fairly often quoted by him.

175. **ne do no fors of dremes**: pay no heed to dreams.
The full distich is :

> 'Somnia ne cures; nam mens humana quod optans,
>   Dum vigilat, sperat, per somnum cernit ad ipsum.'

184. **youre hele**: your health. A.S. hǽlo. **prow,** profit.

185. **tho herbes**: those, A.S. þã, plural of þæt.

186. **han of hire propretee by kynde**: whose property it is by
nature.

kynde: nature.

Cf. the *Parlement of Foules*, "*Pleynt of Kinde*"; i.e. *Com-
plaint of Nature.*

190. **the sonne in his ascencion**: the sun in spring when
it is rising higher every day and gaining force and power.

Cf. the *Franklin's Tale*:

> 'Phebus was old, and hewed like latoun,
>   That in his hote declinacioun
>   Shoon as the burned gold.'

Also *Squire's Tale*:

> 'In Aries, the choleric hote signe.'

Partlet fears lest her husband who is 'choleric' by disposition
should suffer especially at the 'choleric' time of the year.

192. **a grote**: a fourpenny piece.

193. **ffeuere terciane**: tertian fever: a recurrent fever whose
fits occur every three days.

194. **that may be youre bane**: that may destroy you. A.S.
'bana,' a slayer or murderer.

197. **centaure**: centaury: *Centauria nigra.*

ffumetere: fumitory: *Fumaria officinalis.*

Both these herbs were famous remedies for melancholy.

198. **ellebor**: hellebore; *Helleborus niger*. **Cf.** Spenser, 'black hellebore.'

Black hellebore was renowned as a remedy for melancholy; white hellebore was of a different kind.

199. **katapuce**: caper-spurge.

gaitrys beryis: goat's berries, apparently the berries of the buckthorn, *Rhamnus catharticus.*

200. **herbe yue**: probably ground-ivy.

ther mery is: apparently ironical as the plant is nauseous to taste.

202. **for youre fader kyn**: for the sake of your father's race, *i.e.* to do credit to your family.

'Fader' had in A.S. no 's' for the genitive.

204. **graunt mercy**: best thanks, a French phrase.

of youre loore: for your instruction and advice.

205. **Daun Catoun**: daun is used as a term of reverence, often applied to learned men, authors or priests. Cf. Tennyson, 'Dan Chaucer the first warbler.'

Catoun is the Dionysius Cato already referred to.

210. **so moot I thee**: so may I thrive. A.S. þēon, to thrive.

211. **al the reuers seyn of this sentence**: who hold the opposite opinion.

216. **Ther nedeth make of this noon argument**: There is no need to discuss this at length.

217. **The verray preeue**, etc.: the evidence shows it to be true.

218. **Oon of the gretteste auctours.** Cicero in the treatise *De Divinatione.* See Introduction III.

219. **two felawes**: two friends or companions. Cf. the modern usage in the phrase 'Fellow of a University.'

220. **ful good entente**: with good or reverent intention.

223. **so streit of herbergage**: accommodation was so limited. Herbergage is the same word as the modern harbourage; in A.S. it means any place of refuge. This explanation of the separation of the two voyagers is Chaucer's own. Cicero says that one went to lodge with friends.

227. **departen compaignye**: part company. The phrase in the marriage service 'till death us do part' was originally 'till death us depart.'

8   w c

231. **ffer in a yeerd** : far off in a yard. Ffer ought, strictly speaking, to be the comparative as it has a mutated vowel.

oxen of the plough : in Chaucer's time ploughing was performed mainly with oxen as it still is in Italy. Cf. *Knight's Tale* :

> 'I have, God woot, a large field to ere
> And wayke been the oxen in my plough.'

233. **his auenture** : his chance.

239. **ther I lye** : where I lye.

242. **abrayde** : started up, awoke. A.S. abregdan.

244. **took of this no keepe** : paid no heed to it.

245. **Hym thoughte** : it seemed to him. M. methinks. A.S. þyncan, to seem, an impersonal verb.

nas but : was not but, was only.

250. **in the morwe tyde** : in the morning. A.S. morgen.

253. **ful priuely** : secretly.

254. **Do thilke carte arresten** : cause the cart to be stopped. 'Do' with the infinitive of a verb is regularly used in the sense of 'cause.'

255. **sooth** : truth. A.S. sōþ ; in A.S. the word 'sooth' is regularly applied to truth in words, while 'truth' is applied to truth in deeds, faith, or loyalty.

256. **tolde hym euery point** : told him in every detail.

260. **his felawes in** : his friend's lodging. In Chaucer 'in' is used for any kind of dwelling-house but here its meaning is the same as in modern English.

263. **hostiler** : innkeeper. Cf. *Prologue* :

> 'And everich hostiler and tappestere.'

anon : immediately, at once.

268. **ne lenger** : no longer; A.S. lengra.

wolde he lette : would he delay. A.S. lettan, hinder, procrastinate.

271. **arrayed** : arranged or ordered.

272. **deuyse** : tell or describe.

276. **gapyng upright** : lying flat on his back with his mouth open. 'Upright' seems to be often used in the sense of horizontal. Cp. *Reve's Tale* :

> 'This wenche lay upright and faste slepte.'

And also *Knight's Tale* :

> 'The colde deeth, with mouth gapyng upright.'

277. **ministres** : magistrates.

279. **Harrow** : a cry for help. O.F. Haro.

281. **out sterte** : started up.

285. **biwreyest** : biwreyan, to disclose or reveal.

287. **wlatsom** : heinous, abominable. A.S. wlatian, to feel nausea.

289. **heled be** : be concealed. A.S. helan, to conceal or cover. Cf. 'Hela,' the goddess of the lower world and also 'hell,' the concealed or covered-in place.

293. **hent the carter** : seized or laid hold upon him. A.S. hentan, to seize.

pyned : tortured. A.S. pin, torment or torture, from Lat. poena.

294. **engyned** : racked. The word 'engyn' really means any mechanical contrivance ; we have it in modern 'engine' and also in 'gin,' a trap.

295. **biknewe** : acknowledged or confessed.

2 6. **an-hanged by the nekke bon.** Cf. the *Prioresses Tale* :
> 'My throte is cut unto my nekke-boon
> Seyde this child.'

299. **the next chapitre** : it is, as a matter of fact, in the one preceding. See Introduction III.

300. **I gabbe nat** : I am not lying or speaking falsely ; the word also means to chatter idly.

301. **Two men.** Cicero makes Simonides the hero of this tale but Chaucer has altered it considerably, apparently quoting from memory. See Introduction III.

305. **That stood ful myrie,** etc. : was pleasantly situated upon the side of a harbour.

307. **as hem leste** : as it pleased them. A.S. lystan, an impersonal verb.

308. **Iolif** : happy, in good spirits.

309. **casten hem** : planned. Cf. the *Monk's Tale*, 'De Julio Cesare' :
> 'And cast the place, in which he sholde dye.'

312. **a wonder dreem** : a wonderful dream. For the use of 'wonder' as an adj. cf. *Troilus and Criseyde* I. 419:
> 'Allas, what is this wonder maladye.'

agayn the day : towards morning.

315. **wende** : go or journey. A.S. wendan, to turn.

316. **dreynt** : drowned, p.p. of drenchan, to drown. A.S. drencan. The word is really the causative of drincan, to drink, and is employed in its correct sense in the modern phrase ' drenching horses.'

318. **viage** : journey.

319. **As for that day** : so far as concerned that day.

321. **scornéd him ful faste** : heaped scorn upon him.

323. **my thynges** : my business. Cf. *Prologue* :

'Therto he coude endyte and make a thing,'
where ' thing ' means a legal document.

325. **japes** : deceits or jests. Cf. *Miller's Tale* :

' And al his ernest turneth til a jape.'

327. **many a maze** : many a bewildering thing.

330. **forslewthen** : waste away in sloth. In A.S. and Chaucer the prefix ' for ' is generally employed as an intensive in a bad sense.

334. **Noot** : ne woot : I know not.

335. **casuelly** : by chance, as it happened.

340. **maistow leere** : thou mayest learn.

341-2. **to recchelees Of dremés** : too careless about dreams. A.S. recelēas. Cf. the *Hous of Fame*, 668, ' Cupido, the reccheles.'

344. **Seint Kenelm.** The story of Saint Kenelm is told in the *Golden Legend* : he was king of a great stretch of country including many shires ; his father Kenulf died in the year of our Lord 819. Kenelm was made king when he was only seven years of age. Quendred, one of his sisters, turned to wickedness and envied and hated her brother. ' She let make a strong poison and gave it to her brother. But God kept him that it never grieved him. And when she saw that she could not prevail against the king in that manner she laboured to seduce Askeberd, which was chief ruler about the king, and promised to him a great sum of money... if he would slay this young king her brother, and anon they accorded in this treason. And in this while and at that same time, this young holy king was asleep, and dreamed a marvellous dream. For him seemed that he saw a tree stand by his bedside, and that the height thereof touched heaven, and it shined as bright as gold, and had fair branches full of blossoms and fruit. And on every

branch of this tree were tapers of wax burning and lamps alight, which was a glorious sight to behold. And him thought that he climbed upon this tree and Askeberd his governor stood beneath and hewed down this tree that he stood on. And when this tree was falled down, this holy young king was heavy and sorrowful, and him thought there came a fair bird which flew up to heaven with much joy. And anon after this dream he awoke and was all abashed of this dream, which anon after, he told to his nurse named Wolweline. And when he had told to her all his dream she was full heavy and told to him what it meant, and said his sister and the traitor Askeberd had falsely conspired his death.' (Caxton's *Golden Legend.*)

The nurse further explains every detail of his dream, that the bird which flew up to heaven typified his soul. Soon after Askeberd takes Kenelm out with him and murders him and buries his body by a wood called Clent: 'And anon the soul was borne up to heaven in likeness of a white dove.' The narrative goes on to explain how the murder was revealed by a miracle and the body taken up and laid in a shrine with great honour ; in the place where the body had lain there sprang up a fair well 'where much people have been healed of divers sicknesses and maladies.'

Queen Quendred, of course, came to an evil end.

349. **euery deel**: every part or portion, every detail of his dream.

350-1. **to kepe hym weel ffor traison**: to guard himself well against treason.

yeer: a neuter noun in A.S. and unchanged for the plural.

352. **litel tale hath he toold**: he paid but little heed to any dream.

357-8. **Macrobeus, that writ the avision In Affrike of the worthy Cipion**. This is not quite correct ; the *Somnium Scipionis* was written by Cicero and is really an adaptation of Plato's dream of 'Er the Armenian.' Macrobius wrote a long commentary upon the *Somnium Scipionis*. Chaucer was well aware of the true authorship and wrote a summary of the *Somnium* as a Proem to the *Parlement of Foules* where he styles the book : *Tullyus, of the Dreem of Scipioun.*

Macrobius, the commentator, was well known to the men of Chaucer's day and greatly valued as a leading authority upon dreams; he discusses different kinds of dreams and their respective values; some are mere 'insomnia' which have no meaning: 'Hinc insomnio nomen, non quia per somnum videtur (hoc enim est huic generi commune cum caeteris) sed quia in ipso somnio tantummodo esse creditur dum videtur: post somnium nullam sui utilitatem, vel significationem relinquit.'

He then quotes as an example of such 'insomnia' the dreams which terrify Dido.

The true 'visio' is of a different kind; it remains in the mind after waking and has a real meaning. As, for instance, if a dead man appears in a vision and tells his friend of some money which he has hidden in a safe place. A dream is not a true 'somnium' unless it has a sensible meaning; such 'somnia' are, very often, of prophecies or warnings. Macrobius divides them into various types: 'proprium' those which affect a man's own self, 'publicum' those which concern the state, etc. etc.

360. that men after seen: not all dreams but only those which are true visions.

362. of Daniel. Probably alluding to the two dreams of Nebuchadnezzar, the second one signifying his terrible degradation. 'And they shall drive thee from men and thy dwelling shall be with the beasts of the field; they shall make thee to eat grass as oxen' (Daniel iv. 25).

364. Reed eek of Joseph. Cf. *Book of the Duchesse*:

> 'No, not Joseph, withoute drede,
>
> Of Egypte, he that redde so,
>
> The kinges meting Pharao,
>
> No more than coude the leste of us;
>
> Ne nat scarsly Macrobeus
>
> He that wroot al th' avisioun
>
> That he mette, king Scipioun.'

Who interpreted the dream of King Pharaoh.

Cf. also *Hous of Fame* (ii. 6—9). The poet says his dream so wonderful:

> 'That I saye ne Scipioun,
>
> Ne kyng Nabugodonosor,
>
> Pharo, Turnus, ne Elcanor,
>
> Ne mette swich a dreem as this.

370. **seken actes of** sondry remes : search the histories of different kingdoms.

372. **Cresus, that was of Lyde kyng.** Cf. *Hous of Fame* (104–8) :

> 'Lo ! with swich a conclusioun
> As had of his avisioun
> Cresus, that was king of Lyde,
> That high upon a gebet dyde.'

There is also an account of Cresus given in the *Monk's Tale* :

> 'And eek a swevene upon a nyght he mette.

> .   .   .   .   .

> Upon a tree he was, as that hym thoughte,
> Ther Juppiter hym wesshe, bothe bak and syde
> And Phebus eek a fair towaille hym broughte
> To dryen hym with, and therfore wex his pryde;
> And to his doghter, that stood him bisyde,
> Which that he knew in heigh science habounde,
> He bad hire telle him what it signyfyde,
> And she his dreem bigan right thus expounde :
> "The tree " quod she "the galwes is to meene ;
> And Juppiter bitokneth snow and reyn,
> And Phebus with his towaille so clene,
> Tho been the sonne-bemes for to seyn ;
> Thou shalt anhanged be, fader, certeyn,
> Reyn shal thee wasshe and sonne shal thee drye."'

The Nun's Priest, in referring to Cresus, is really quoting the tale of the previous narrator.

375. **Lo heere Andromacha :** the dream of Andromache is not to be found in the *Iliad* but in Dares Phrygius ; the latter was a mediaeval author whose book purported to be an account of the siege of Troy written by a contemporary on the Trojan side ; the men of Chaucer's time seem to have taken Dares at his surface value and regarded him as superior to Homer because more accurate. Chaucer refers to him in the *Hous of Fame* :

> 'And by him stood, withouten lees,
> Ful wonder hye on a pileer
> Of yren, he, the gret Omeer;
> And with him Dares.'   (146, 4—7.)

He goes on to say that there is a 'little envy' among these different writers and that ' Omere ' is too favourable to the Greeks:

> 'Oon seyde that Omere made lyes,
>   Feyninge in his poetries,
>   And was to Grekes favorable.'

378. lorne : p.p. of the verb 'lose.' A.S. lēosan, loren.

381. natheles : none the less.

384. I may nat dwelle : I cannot discuss longer.

386. Avision: 'visio' is the word used by Macrobius to signify the truly prophetic dream as distinguished from the one which is only a false appearance.

388. ne telle…no stoor : I value as nothing.

391. stynte al this : cease speaking of all this.

397–8. In principio Mulier est hominis confusio. This is a sentence from Vincent of Beauvais, *Speculum Historiale* (x. 71). According to the narrative the emperor Hadrian consults a certain philosopher named Secundus who has taken a vow of silence and will not speak, even to the emperor ; however he consents to write answers to questions and in reply to the question 'What is woman ? ' he responds with this phrase. Chauntecleer quotes the sentence in revenge for Partlet's sarcasm but, of course, fearing to offend her, mistranslates.

399. sentence : meaning. Cf. *Prologue*, Clerk of Oxford :

> ' Noght o word spak he more than was nede
>   And that was seyd in forme and reverence,
>   And short and quik and ful of hy sentence.'

406. word : speech or sentence.

407. eke : also : A.S. ēac.

414. toos. Chaucer sometimes uses the strong and sometimes the weak plural for this noun.

419. in his pasture : feeding.

422. That highte March : in Chaucer's time the New Year was counted from March 25th ; the creation of the world was popularly supposed to have taken place at the vernal equinox.

423–4. passed were also Syn March bigan thritty dayes and two : the date meant is, apparently, May 3rd. See Introduction III.

428. Taurus : the sun enters Taurus in the middle of April and remains there until the middle of May.

430. **kynde**: by nature.

431. **it was pryme**: 9 o'clock: the end of the first quarter of the day; the day was counted from 6 a.m. to 6 p.m.

441. **a rethor**: a rhetorician.

endite: dictate or write. Cf. *Prologue*, Squire:

> 'He koude songes make and wel endite.'

446. **Launcelot de Lake**: the contemptuous tone of this reference is noteworthy. See Introduction III.

449. **A colfox**: a fox with black markings: col = coal.

450. **wonned**: dwelt. A.S. wunian, to dwell.

451. **forn-cast**: premeditated.

455. **wortes**: plants or vegetables; the *Roman de Renart* says cabbages, which is probably what Chaucer means. 'Wort' is still left in a corrupted form in the word 'orchard' and also in botanical names such as St John's wort, milk-wort, etc.

456. **vndren**: lit. the intervening period; it seems to mean here the middle of the morning, about 10.30 or 11. It can also mean the mid-afternoon.

459. **liggen**: lie. A.S. licgan.

461. **Scariot**: Judas Iscariot.

Genylon: the traitor who caused the defeat of Charlemagne and the death of Roland. Cf. the *Book of the Duchesse* (1121):

> 'the false Genelon,
>
> He that purchased the treason
>
> Of Rowland and of Olivere.'

462. **dissimulour**: deceiver, traitor.

Greek Synon: the man who caused the wooden horse to be brought into Troy and so entailed the destruction of the city. Chaucer refers to him also in the *Hous of Fame* (151-6):

> 'First saw I the destruccioun
>
> Of Troye, through the Greek Sinoun,
>
> That with his false forsweringe,
>
> And his chere and his lesinge
>
> Made the hors broght into Troye,
>
> Thorgh which Troyens lost al hir joye.'

Virgil's reference is:

> 'fatisque deum defensus iniquis
>
> Inclusos utero Danaos et pinea furtim
>
> Laxat claustra Sinon.' (*Aen.* II. 257-9.)

468. forwoot : knows before : the 'foresciti' of Wyclif. See Introduction III.

nedes : of necessity.

469. After the opinion : according to the opinion.

certein clerkis : men of learning.

470. parfit clerk : accomplished scholar. Cf. the *Prologue* :
    ' He was a verray parfit gentil knight.'

471. in scole : in the schools of philosophy. Chaucer is probably thinking of Wyclif.

The question of 'predestination' was one of the chief philosophical problems of the day. See Introduction I, III.

474. bulte it to the bren : sift it thoroughly.

475. Augustyn : who discussed the question of predestination.

476. Boece. Chaucer's favourite philosopher ; Chaucer translated the *Consolatio Philosophiæ*, one of the noblest works available in the Middle Ages, and he often refers to it and quotes from it in his poems, particularly in *Troilus and Criseyde*. Boethius was put to death by the emperor Theodoric. See Introduction II. Cf. *Troilus* (IV. 967):

    ' But nathelees, allas ! whom shal I leve?
    For ther ben grete clerkes many oon,
    That destinee thorugh argumentes preve ;
    And som men seyn that nedely ther is noon ;
    But that free chois is yeven us everichoon.
    O, welawey ! so sleye arn clerkes olde,
    That I not whos opinion I may holde.'

Bisshope Bradwardyn. Thomas Bradwardine, author of a work entitled *De Causa Dei* ; he died in 1349, a victim to the black death, just after having been appointed Archbishop of Canterbury. He had previously been Divinity Professor and Chancellor of the University of Oxford. Wyclif proclaimed himself as a follower of Augustine and a successor in philosophy to Bradwardine. See Introduction III.

477. worthy forwityng : true foreknowledge : Wyclif's 'foresciti.'

483. Or if his wityng streyneth, etc. : or if his knowledge does not compel except by conditional necessity.

490. Wommennes conseils been ful ofte colde : a popular proverb.

coldo : baneful or fatal.

497. **Rede auctours**: the 'authors' who wrote against women were mainly monastic writers such as those quoted by the Wife of Bath: Jerome against Jovinian: Valery and Theophrast, etc.

503. **Agayn the sonne**: in the sunlight.

505. **Phisiologus.** Chaucer probably refers to a book in Latin metre entitled *Physiologus de Naturis xii Animalium* by Theobaldus. It contains a chapter entitled 'De Sirenis' which explains how the sirens sing beautifully and lure sailors by their voices.

511. **cride anon, 'Cok, cok'**: probably meant only as a cry of alarm.

514. **ffro his contrarie**: from his natural enemy, as chickens cower at the sight of the hawk.

521. **vileynye**: harm or wrong.

528. **Boece**: this is probably a reference to the treatise *De Musica*. The explanation of the nature of sound-waves given in the *Hous of Fame* (781—820) seems also to be quoted from the same source.

529. **My lord youre fader.** In the *Roman de Renart* the fox claims relationship to Chanteclin, father of Chantecler. Chaucer's amendment is much more plausible.

534. **So moote I brouke**: so may I retain the use or sight. A.S. brūcan, to use or employ.

543. **discrecion**: wisdom.

546. **Daun Burnel the Asse**: this was the famous mediaeval satire the *Speculum Stultorum* or *Mirror of Fools* by Nigellus Wereker, precentor of Canterbury in the latter half of the twelfth century. The hero of the book is a certain ass called Burnellus (*i.e.* the Brown) who is dissatisfied with the length of his tail and travels to various medical schools seeking advice. On his way to Paris he falls in with a fellow-traveller who tells him the story to which Chaucer refers; the holder of a certain benefice had a son named Gundulf who once, by carelessness, struck a young chicken with a rod he carried and broke its leg. The young cock cherished feelings of revenge and, after several years, his opportunity arrived. Gundulf had been promised his father's benefice and the day of consecration was fixed; he was to set out early in the morning. The cock heard the arrangement and exulted; when his time for crowing arrived he made no sound, knowing well that the house-

hold, relying upon him, would oversleep themselves. Gundulf,
when he at length awoke, hurried to the city but it was too late, he
had lost his benefice; his parents died shortly afterwards and
Gundulf was turned away from his old home and became a
beggar.

549. **yong and nyce** : young and delicate.

553. **his subtiltee** : the cunning of the cock in *Burnellus*.

554. **for seinte charitee** : a French phrase.

555. **countrefete** : imitate or rival your father.

556. **gan to bete** : to beat his wings together.

559. **flatour** : flatterer.

560. **losengeour** : flatterer, deceiver.

563. **Ecclesiaste** : Ecclesiasticus xii. 10, 11.

567. **for the nones** : for the nonce : employed generally as a
rhyming tag.

568. **Russell** : the red one. In the *Roman de Renart* this
name is given to the son of Renart.

569. **gargat** : throat.

571. **sewed** : pursued or followed.

574. **ne roghte nat** : cared nothing for. A.S. reccan, rohte.

575. **on a Friday** : supposed to be an unlucky day; it is still a
superstition not to commence a journey or any other important
adventure upon Friday.

580. **on thy day to dye** : Friday was sacred to Venus.

581. **Gaufred** : Geoffrey de Vinsauf who lived at the end of
the twelfth and the beginning of the thirteenth century. He was
the author of a treatise on the poetic art called *Nova Poetria*,
written in hexameter verse. He teaches the art of composition in
poetry with illustrative examples, one of these being a lament for the
death of Richard I ; he 'chides' the Friday because on that day
Richard received the arrow-wound from which he died.

> 'Mors non fuit ejus,
> Sed tua, non una, sed publica mortis origo.
> O Veneris lacrimosa dies ! O sydus amarum !
> Illa dies tua nox fuit, et Venus illa venenum,' etc.

See also Introduction III.

583. **With shot** : Richard I was wounded by an arrow while
conducting a siege in Normandy.

584. **thy sentence, and thy loore**: thy wisdom and thy learning.

590. **Ylion**: Troy. It is possible that Chaucer understood by Ilion not the whole city but the citadel in its midst. Thus in the *Hous of Fame* he describes how the wooden horse is brought into the city:

> 'And after this was grave, allas !
> How Ilioun assailed was
> And wonne, and king Priam y-slayn,
> Despitously of dan Pirrus.
> And next that saw I how Venus
> Whan that she saw the *castel* brende.'

591. **streite swerd**: drawn or naked sword.

592. **hent kyng Priam by the berd.** Chaucer seems to be quoting from memory as his details are not exact. Virgil describes how Pyrrhus pursues Polites, the son of Priam, and slays him at the altar by which Priam had taken refuge ; the old man rebukes him for his impiety and attacks him ; Pyrrhus seizes him *by the hair* and slays him :

> ' Hoc dicens altaria ad ipsa trementem
> Traxit et in multo lapsantem sanguine nati,
> Implicuitque comam laeva, dextraque coruscum
> Extulit ac lateri capulo tenus abdidit ensem.'

(Aen. II.)

597. **Hasdrubales wyf**: the wife of Hasdrubal king of Carthage ; the Romans burnt it B.C. 146.

601. **wilfully** : deliberately.

604. **Nero brende the citee.** Cf. the *Monk's Tale*, ' Nero ' :

> ' He Rome brende for his delicacye (caprice).
> The senatoures he slow upon a day
> To here how men wolde wepe and crye.'

609. **sely** : poor or innocent. A.S. sǣlig, happy or blessed.

612. **syen** : saw. A.S. sāwon.

614. **weylaway** : alas !

616. **staues** : sticks.

618. **Malkyn** : a common name for a maid-servant.

624. **as men wolde hem quelle** : as if they were about to be killed. A.S. cwellan, to slay.

627. **benedicitee** : pronounced as three syllables ben'dic'te.

628. **Iakke Straw** : one of the leaders in the Peasants' Rebellion 1381.

meynee : followers. A.S. manig, a number of people, a retinue.

630. **any Flemyng** : the Flemish weavers. See Introduction I.

632. **bemes** : trumpets. A.S. bēam, tree, pointing to the fact that they were originally made of wood.

box : boxwood.

633. **powped** : blew hard.

634. **howped** : M.E. whoop.

642. **as wys** : as certainly.

643. **Turneth** : imp. plural.

646. **Maugree youre heed** : in spite of all you can do. Fr. malgré.

647. **in feith** : certainly, deliberately.

650. **delyuerly** : quickly or swiftly. Cf. *Prologue*, Squire : ' And wonderly deliver and greet of strengthe.'

657. **of no wikke entente** : with no evil intention.

666. **Al wilfully** : deliberately.

neuere thee : A.S. þēon, to thrive.

668. **vndiscreet of gouernaunce** : lacking in self-control.

669. **jangleth** : chatters, talks.

676. **To oure doctrine** : for our instruction.

GLOSSARY

abrayde : started up, awaked
attamed : broached or began
attempree : moderate
avauntour : boaster
aventure : chance or fortune

batailled : embattled
bemes : trumpets
biknewe : confessed
biwreyest : betrayest
brend : burnt
brouke : enjoy, use
bulte : boult or sift
burned : burnished

cas : fortune, chance
casten : planned, intended
catel : property, chattels
certes : certainly
cleped : called or named
colera : choleric humour
colfox : brant-fox, with black markings
compaignable : courteous
compleccioun : bodily habit, constitution

debonaire : gracious, meek
deel : part or portion
departen : part
delyverly : adroitly
devyse : tell
dissymulour : deceiver
drecched : harassed or troubled
dreynt : drowned

erst : previously
engyned : racked or tortured
ey : egg

faren : gone
flatour : flatterer
forn-cast : predestined

fors : force ; **no fors**, no matter
forwityng : foreknowledge
free : generous

gabbe : to lie
gaitrys-beryis : berries of the dog-wood tree
gargat : throat
grote : fourpenny-piece

hele : health or advantage
heled : concealed
hente : seized, laid hold of
hertelees : a coward
highte or **heet** : was called or named
hostiler : innkeeper
housbondrie : economy

jangleth : chatters
japes : tricks, mockeries

katapuce : spurge
keen : kine
keepe : heed
kynde : nature

lemes : gleams, flashes
leste or **liste** : it pleased
lette : hindered
liggen : lie
lite : little, short time
lith : joint or limb
lorne : lost
losengeour : flatterer

maugre your heed : in spite of all you can do
maze : confused thing
mette : dreamt
meynee : followers
ministres : magistrates

natheles : none the less
nyce : delicate, tender

orlogge : sundial or clock

paramours : wives or sweet-hearts
prime : time between 6 and 9 a.m.
prow : profit
pyned : tortured

quelle : kill

real : royal
recche : interpret or expound
recchelees : careless
remes : realms, kingdoms
rente : income
replecciouns : excesses
rethor : rhetorician
roghte : cared

secree : secret
sely : simple, innocent
sentence : meaning or eloquence
sewed : followed
seynd : singed or broiled
shente : injured, spoilt
shrewe : curse
shrighte : shrieked

smal : narrow
stape : advanced
stevene : voice
streyneth : constrains or compels
stynte : cease
swevene : dream
syen : saw

terciane : recurring every third day, intermittent
thee or **theen** : thrive
tool : weapon

undren : morning, time between 9 a.m. and noon
upright : full length, whether standing or lying

whilom : once upon a time, formerly
wight : man or person
wilfully : deliberately
wlatsom : loathsome
wonned : dwelt
woot : knows
wortes : plants, vegetables
worthy : noble

ywis : certainly, assuredly